Youth Sunday School for a New Century

Chuck Gartman
and Richard Barnes

LifeWay Press
Nashville, Tennessee

ISBN 0-7673-9984-6
This book is a resource for courses numbered LS-0025, LS0068
for the ministry area "Sunday School Leadership" of the Christian Growth Study Plan.

Dewey Decimal Classification number 268.433
Subject Heading: Sunday Schools—Youth

Printed in the United States of America
Available from Customer Service Center 1-800-458-2772 and LifeWay Christian Stores

Youth Ministry Services Section
Youth Sunday School Ministry Department
Sunday School Group
LifeWay Christian Resources of the Southern Baptist Convention
127 Ninth Avenue, North
Nashville, Tennessee 37234-0174

Acknowledgments: Scripture quotations marked NIV
are from the Holy Bible, New International Version
copyright 1973, 1978, 1984
by International Bible Society

Contents

The Writers

Chuck Gartman's name is well-known in the Southern Baptist Convention. A 30-year veteran of youth ministry, he is a graduate of Howard Payne University and Southwestern Baptist Theological Seminary, and has served churches in Texas and Tennessee.

Chuck wrote *The Potential Youth Sunday School Workers Manual* and he has written many articles for LifeWay publications. His hobbies include racquetball, basketball, reading, collecting mugs, eagles, tiger pictures, and eating Blue Bell ice cream.

Chuck, his wife Connie, and their three daughters, Brandie, Brittany, and Brooklyn live in Franklin, Tennessee, where he is 12th Grade Director at First Baptist Church. He is the Manager of the Youth Ministry Services Section of the Youth Sunday School Ministry Department at LifeWay Christian Resources.

Richard Barnes's first youth leadership position was as a student summer missionary in 1969 in Honolulu, Hawaii (somebody had to do it!). A graduate of Dallas Baptist University and Southwestern Baptist Theological Seminary, he went on to serve churches in Connecticut and Texas while writing curriculum for Youth Sunday School and Youth Discipleship Training. Richard came to LifeWay Christian Resources in 1985 as editor of *Youth in Action* and currently serves as the Director of the Youth Sunday School Ministry Department.

Richard and his wife Mary enjoy walking in the beautiful Tennessee hills and hiking in the majestic Rocky Mountains. They have two grown sons, Stephen who is married to Miranda, and Philip who is married to Laura. Like Chuck, Richard is a member of First Baptist Church, Franklin, Tennesee, where he and his wife work with high school youth in Sunday School.

Foreword

It was time. The world He had created had chosen its own way and was hopelessly lost. God had a strategy that would transform the world—one that would replace fear with faith, despair with hope, hatred with love, spiritual darkness with light.

God chose to enter the kingdom of this world personally, in Jesus Christ, transforming forever anyone who would receive Him. The kingdom of this world was intersected, once and for all, by the kingdom of God. Through Jesus, God overcame sin and death with His righteousness and eternal life.

Jesus demonstrated God's love for all people. His life and ministry were a living portrait of perfect love. Jesus demonstrated this love by obediently fulfilling God's strategy to reconcile a lost world to Himself. Jesus willingly submitted His life as a sacrifice, through death on a cross, to free each of us from the ultimate penalty for our sin. Jesus made a way for us to receive abundant, eternal life. Everything about Jesus revealed God's strategy to act.

Jesus' mission extends to all of His disciples throughout time. He has called us to continue His work, and He has equipped us for that work (Matt. 28:18-20). We are to be transformed people. We are to be agents of transformation.

Sunday School is the strategy that can engage people in Great Commission ministry, leading them to faith in the Lord Jesus Christ and building Great Commission Christians. Sunday School must stay firmly grounded in God's living and written Word. However, there is more to Sunday School for a new century than gathering for Bible study, as important as that is.

In the 21st century, Sunday School must provide seven-day-a-week opportunities to grow in understanding of and in obedience to God's Word. Sunday School must provide opportunities for people to express their love for God and for people by engaging them in ministry and missions. It must build unity and fellowship in the church, and help people find ways to express their love for God in all that they do.

It is time. It is time because of the opportunities. Today, churches have a wonderful opportunity to fulfill the Lord's command. The new world of the 21st century and the third millennium is not unlike the world God entered when He divided time forever with Jesus' birth. Our world, continuing to choose its own way, remains hopelessly lost without Christ. It is time because of the overwhelming need.

The mission and ministry of Christ was God's strategy from the beginning. His strategy is ours. Your time is now.

Bill Taylor

Introduction

A Vision for the 21st Century

By Richard Barnes

The kingdom of heaven is like a mustard seed, which a man took and planted in his field. Though it is the smallest of all your seeds, yet when it grows, it is the largest of garden plants and becomes a tree, so that the birds of the air come and perch in its branches (Matt. 13:31-32).

During the last decade of the 20th century, we have witnessed remarkable movements of God in the lives of teenagers. As we cross the threshold of the 21st century, reflect on the kingdom of God—where God is moving in the lives of this generation. Can you spot where youth you know have been involved in or touched by:

• A growing movement of prayer? Two expressions of God's kingdom work are in the campus club movement and See You at the Pole. On September 16, 1998, the ninth annual See You at the Pole event saw an estimated three million teenagers gather around flagpoles to pray for their schools, communities, and countries. Now an international movement, See You at the Pole has spread to at least 15 countries beyond the United States, including Australia, Ghana, Japan, Singapore, South Korea, and Turkey.[1]

• A continually expanding commitment to moral purity? This simple grassroots pledge by youth to remain sexually abstinent until marriage is seen most clearly in the True Love Waits campaign that began in 1993 in a single Tennessee church. By 1999 True Love Waits had garnered support from 80 denominations and spread to more than 60 nations internationally. True Love Waits leaders project as many as 750,000 teenagers have taken pledges stating that true love does indeed wait.[2]

• A hands-on involvement in missions at home and abroad? The willingness of this generation to take the gospel to the world is likely unparalleled in previous generations. Every year during the 1990s increasing tens of thousands of students served in North American Mission Board (NAMB) short-term projects, International Mission Board (IMB) trips, Acteens Activators and Acteens Activators Abroad, and state Baptist convention partnerships. Add to this new LifeWay international Centrifuge and M-fuge camps and international World Changers projects. Then add the scores of local church national and international missions trips. Finally, add many non-denominational national and international missions trips. One leader of international youth missions teams summarizes, "We've got the Lord's invitation because every Christian is called to the 'ends of the earth.'[3]"

• A growing concern for expanding the kingdom of God, personal evangelism, and spiritual awakening? In a national meeting in January 1999 youth leaders from many denominations and evangelical youth ministries, including Southern Baptists, cited evidences of a spiritual awakening in this generation. Today's youth, they said, are noted for their passion for prayer, worship, moral purity, and student servant leadership. Henry Blackaby has observed that much of the significant evangelism emerging in American churches is being born and carried out by youth and students.[4] A key element in spiritual awakening can be seen in YouthLink 2000, a gathering of more than 100,000 SBC youth in seven different cities (December 28-31, 1999); a once-in-a-lifetime event designed to unite a generation of Christian youth as they moved into the new millennium.

There's More...

Yes, there's more evidence of the kingdom of God at work. Consider these real-life reports from youth involved in Sunday Schools throughout the United States:

- Evangelism: A youth and Youth Sunday School teacher share their joy in leading a youth to Christ on their very first night of FAITH Sunday School Evangelism training.
- Discipleship: A high school student emails his teacher affirming the Bible study on the previous Sunday.
- Fellowship: A student who first hated moving to her new community finds fellowship and friendship through students who visit in her home and befriend her at school.
- Ministry: A Youth Sunday School teacher prayerfully ministers to the class as the students deal with the suicide of a member's father.
- Worship: A youth writes the editor of *essential connection* magazine stating how often God has used the daily devotional magazine to speak to her.

These Youth Sunday School testimonies represent multiplied thousands of individuals whom God touches every week through the ministry of small-group Bible studies we call Youth Sunday School. In the kingdom of God, the small group, with the individual teachers and students in them, is a strategic part of His work. Individuals and small groups may feel like "mustard seeds" compared to the larger, sweeping movements of God, but to the youth involved in Youth Sunday School, that Youth department and class are God's kingdom come to them.

Critical Questions for Youth Sunday School in the New Century

- As Youth Sunday School moves into the 21st century, to what extent will God be able to work through its leaders and participants to extend His kingdom?
- If God sends a great spiritual awakening in this generation, will Youth Sunday School leaders and learners be *prepared* to *encounter* God's Word in Bible study groups committed to *continue* learning and living for Christ daily in all relationships, including the family?
- What must Youth Sunday School be and do in the 21st century?

These are big questions that this book intends to tackle!

A New Definition

Let's begin by stating the driving force for Sunday School, the Great Commission.

Then Jesus came to them and said, "All authority in heaven and on earth has been given to me. Therefore go and make disciples of all nations, baptizing them in the name of the Father and of the Son and of the Holy Spirit and teaching them to obey everything I have commanded you. And surely I am with you always, to the very end of the age (Matt. 28:18-20).

Youth Sunday School seeks to fulfill the Great Commission by making disciples who are Great Commission Christians; that is, believers who seek to obey everything Jesus commanded. The Great Commandment, Jesus declared, was to love God and love one's neighbor as oneself (Matt. 22:37-40). And the proof of love for God is obedience to His commands (John 14:15).

To position Youth Sunday School to be in step with God's kingdom work in the world and in the churches, examine carefully this new definition of Sunday School for the 21st century:

Sunday School is the foundational strategy in a local church for leading people to faith in the Lord Jesus Christ and for building Great Commission Christians through Bible study groups that engage people in evangelism, discipleship, fellowship, ministry, and worship.

Five Strategic Principles

As the "foundational strategy," Youth Sunday School provides the foundation upon which you can build all other church ministries with youth. Consider these five fresh strategic directives for 21st Century Youth Sunday School.

Foundational Evangelism 1

1. The Principle of Foundational Evangelism

Sunday School is the foundational evangelism strategy of the church.

1. Sunday School emphasizes ongoing, open Bible study groups that reproduce new groups as the best long-term approach for building a ministry environment that guides preschoolers and children toward conversion through foundational teaching, encourages unsaved people to come to faith in Christ, assimilates new believers into the life of the church, and encourages believers to lead others to Christ.
2. Sunday School provides the most efficient churchwide evangelism training network to equip members to become passionate soul-winners.
3. Sunday School encourages Bible study in short-term groups and through special Bible teaching events as effective ways to promote outreach and evangelism and to address specific life concerns, spiritual issues, church functions, and doctrinal issues.
4. Sunday School creates a great center for missionary power as people tell and live the wondrous story of Christ's redeeming love.

Foundational Discipleship 2

2. The Principle of Foundational Discipleship

Sunday School is the seven-day-a-week strategy for involving people in seeking the kingdom of God and fulfilling the Great Commission.

1. Sunday School provides the primary organizational framework for involving families and individuals in the comprehensive work of the church including evangelism, discipleship, fellowship, ministry, and worship.
2. Sunday School is a foundational step of discipleship and encourages members to strengthen their Christian walk by participating in other discipleship opportunities.
3. Sunday School emphasizes that every member who is a believer must become accountable for the responsibility God has given him or her as a minister and missionary to the world.
4. Sunday School supports all other church ministries and intentionally encourages its members to be good stewards, fully involved in the church's overall mission.

3. The Principle of Family Responsibility

Sunday School affirms the home as the center of biblical guidance.

1. Sunday School helps equip Christian parents, including single parents, to fulfill their responsibility as the primary Bible teachers and disciplers of their children.
2. The Sunday School encourages Christian parents who by word and deed guide their children to integrate the Scriptures into their lives influencing how they think and act.
3. Sunday School involves families in the comprehensive work of the church.
4. Sunday School works to nurture sound and healthy families and seeks to lead non-Christian parents to Christ.

4. The Principle of Spiritual Transformation

Sunday School engages learners in the biblical model of instruction that leads to spiritual transformation.

1. Sunday School affirms that spiritual transformation is God's work of changing a believer into the likeness of Jesus by creating a new identity in Christ and by empowering a lifelong relationship of love, trust, and obedience to glorify God.
2. Sunday School champions the absolute truth and authority of the Word of God and compels believers to integrate a biblical worldview into their minds, hearts, and lives through ongoing systematic Bible study.
3. Sunday School recognizes that Bible study is most effective when it occurs in the context of the learner's total life, especially family relationships, and when it considers the special needs, generational perspective, age, life-stage characteristics, and learning styles of the learners.
4. Sunday School addresses transcultural life issues common to individuals, churches, families, tribes, and nations regardless of geographic, ethnic, or language identity.

5. The Principle of Biblical Leadership

Sunday School calls leaders to follow the biblical standard of leadership.

1. Sunday School affirms the pastor as the primary leader in its ministry of building Great Commission Christians.
2. Sunday School calls leaders to a prophetic ministry, listening to God's voice, discerning His message, integrating the message into their lives, and proclaiming His truth through His church to the nations.
3. Sunday School recognizes that the leader is the lesson in that every leader is accountable for being an authentic example of Christianity in personal living and producing new leaders for service through the ministries of the church.
4. Sunday School recognizes that planning is essential to implementing its strategy.

Best Practices

These strategic principles form the foundation for Sunday School as strategy. But to be effective, strategy must move beyond the philosophical and theoretical to the practical. How can the strategy of Sunday School (and Youth Sunday School) be implemented in your church?

The rest of this book deals with the "best practices" of Sunday School. These ten best practices are recommendations for implementing biblical and strategic

Sunday School ministry in the local church. They are rooted in the knowledge of how people and churches work, and they come from observing effective work in a broad base of churches over an extended period of time. In the following chapters and in the appendix of this book, these are some best practices that will be addressed:

1. Identify the Strategy
2. Organize with Purpose
3. Build the Leadership
4. Train Effective Leaders
5. Provide Space and Equipment
6. Value Record Keeping
7. Develop Soul Winners
8. Teach to Transform
9. Conduct Special Events
10. Choose Sound Curriculum

The FAITH Sunday School Evangelism Strategy

What evidence is there that God is using Sunday School to serve as the "foundational strategy in a local church"? One evidence of a fresh moving of God in Sunday School is the FAITH Sunday School Evangelism Strategy.

In January 1998, LifeWay Christian Resources launched the FAITH Sunday School Evangelism Strategy. This simple strategy to reclaim evangelism as the birthright of Sunday School grew from the 20-plus years of experience of doing personal evangelism through the Sunday School at First Baptist Church, Daytona Beach, Florida. Within 12 months the 28 churches who were trained to implement the strategy had grown to more than 1400 churches! Youth leaders have just begun to launch the strategy as they develop Student FAITH teams linking personal evangelism and ministry with Youth Sunday School classes and departments. God appears to be using the FAITH Sunday School Evangelism Strategy to call churches to make disciples through conducting the basic Sunday School functions well: evangelism, discipleship, fellowship, ministry, and worship.

Back to the Future!

As God works through you, implementing the 21st century Sunday School definition, five strategic principles, and ten best practices will set your Youth Sunday School on a new kingdom course. At the same time, you take with you youth Bible study groups, not as an organization, but as a foundational strategy that functions with purpose in five areas: evangelism, discipleship, fellowship, ministry, and worship. Building from these five functions, it's like going back to the future!

[1] "See You at the Pole '98 World Report," National Network of Youth Ministries, Fall, 1998.

[2] Facts and Trends, "True Love Waits Goes to Washington," 1998; confirmed by Nancy Boehmer, 1/25/99.

[3] "Let No One Despise Their Youth," by Norman Miller. *The Commission*, October 1998, 9. [Other sources: Bron Holcomb, IMB, 1/25/99; Chad Childress, NAMB, 1/25/99; Joe Palmer, 1/25/99].

[4] "Sending High School Students Overseas," by Bron Holcomb. *Youth Ministry Update*, February 1999.

[5] *Kingdom Principles for Church Growth*, by O. Eugene Mims.

Chapter 1

Youth Sunday School with Purpose

When I first started out in youth ministry, I didn't have a clue about why we had Youth Sunday School. As youth minister, I stayed busy carrying out the work of my own little kingdom. There were others who took care of Youth Sunday School; I was trying to build a youth ministry centered around me. Consequently, when I left that church after serving it for over a year and a half as a college student, much that had been done was lost because there was no leadership among the adults who worked with teens—the ones who were there long after I left the church.

In looking back, I see that the ministry should have been built on a solid foundation of Bible study, discipleship, missions education, Christian music, and Christian activities. The smart thing would have been to build that ministry around adults who would sustain the ministry to youth when the youth minister was gone.

It has been my contention for many years now that our ministry through the Bible study organization has been and continues to be driven by a systemized plan to reach and teach youth. What we have now is a comprehensive, biblical, and ministry-based purpose for the Sunday School organization of our churches. Understanding our purpose as volunteer Youth Sunday School leaders can give us a freedom of expression that results in us being better leaders for Christ's sake.

→ Understanding our purpose as ministers with youth can give us a freedom of expression that results in being better ministers for Christ's sake.

At the risk of seeming simplistic, consider this outline of purpose that is easily remembered and easily communicated: There are five functions of an effective Youth Sunday School ministry that are scriptural; the overarching authority and method for doing these functions comes from The Great Commission. Thus, we use the terms *Youth Sunday School* or *Youth Bible Study.*

What are those five functions and how do they relate to us as Youth Sunday School leaders? As a Youth Sunday School leader, based on the functions (or purposes) for Youth Sunday School, your ministry includes:

1. Evangelism

Your job is to evangelize youth and the adults who have influence over them—their parents, teachers, friends, work associates, and so on. For me, this is my job description: *I am to bring the claims of Christ to bear on the lives of teenagers so that they have an opportunity to be changed by Christ through salvation. As a leader of teens it is my purpose and responsibility to be a witness to youth. I am to do that by how I live my life as well by the words that I say.* One person I know says that we are to be witnesses visually and verbally.

In the Great Commission (Matt. 28:18-20), the instruction is given that we should make disciples (evangelize people), teaching them to observe everything that God has commanded. Every person may not have the gift of evangelism, but every person is to be a witness of what God has done in his or her life through a personal relationship with Christ.

One survey of Baptist churches several years ago said that growing churches used Sunday School as their primary outreach organizations—Sunday School in the late '90s and into the 21st century will continue to have evangelism at its heart. Thus a person not only can grow as a Christian by studying the Bible, he or she can actually become a Christian by studying the Bible.

The first purpose of Youth Sunday School is to evangelize youth and the adults who influence them.

S.W. PRODUCTIONS

2. Discipleship

Over the years many have placed an enormous amount of emphasis on winning teens to Christ. The focus seems to have been to get kids saved so that they won't have to spend an eternity in hell apart from Christ. There is, of course, that emphasis in the Great Commission; however, to stop there is to cut short the Commission, because the verses in Matthew 28 commission us not only to evangelize, but to disciple. "Make disciples of all nations" and "teaching them to observe all that I have commanded you" go hand-in-hand; these actions don't stand alone. Therefore, we cannot relax after we have witnessed to a youth and he or she has started the Christian pilgrimage from sin to a new life.

What is involved in discipling teens? By definition a *disciple* is *a willing learner.* A disciple could be compared to an apprentice. Following is a list of some of the things we would like teens to learn to do as they grow spiritually in their relationship with the Lord:

- Read, study, memorize, and meditate on God's Word;
- Share their faith with friends and family;
- Understand what is involved in their relationship with God;
- Know what they believe;
- Conduct themselves in a manner that brings honor and glory to their Lord, including being servant leaders.

Before teens can do any of those things, they need to see those actions at work in our lives. We Youth Sunday School leaders are called to be models of the Christian life. So the first step is to continually work toward spiritual maturity ourselves. The leader is the lesson!

Following are some ways we youth leaders can model the Christian life:

- We will be reading, studying, memorizing, and meditating on Scripture as we guide youth to do the same. Using the Bible Study lesson each week is one way of getting teens involved in an ongoing study of Scripture. As we do it, and encourage them to do it, they will begin to have a greater appreciation for God's Word in their lives.
- As we habitually share our faith with friends, our students, and our families, teens will become more comfortable sharing their own faith.
- As we begin to have an understanding of all that we have in our relationship with Christ and act on those things, teens will model our behavior, and begin to live their lives out for Christ as well.

Youth Sunday School leaders are called to be models of the Christian life.

• As we gain greater insight into our Christian beliefs and actively share those beliefs in our Bible Study groups, youth will begin to stretch and ask questions that will shape their own beliefs.

• As we conduct our lives in a way that honors God and as we give our lives in service to others, teens will begin to do the same. Our walk must match our talk!

The second purpose of Youth Sunday School is to disciple teenagers in their relationship with God.

3. Fellowship

What comes to your mind when the word *fellowship* is mentioned? Home, food, fun, games, music, after-church recreation? Those are terms that come to my mind, but none of those is *fellowship* in the biblical sense—they are only steps to true fellowship. Our job as Youth Sunday School workers is to guide teens to fellowship and to provide opportunities for them to experience fellowship as Christian youth.

A helpful definition of *fellowship* is *the intimate relationship among Christians that is only possible because of their relationship with Christ.* The Bible calls it *koinonia.*

As Christian adults working in a Youth Sunday School, we often miss out on times of fellowship with other adults. Even though we may experience genuine *koinonia* with youth, our deepest fellowship will occur when we are spending time with other adults.

Fellowship is developed among Christians as we are honest about our feelings and share what God has done and is doing in our lives. One word of warning however—use discretion when sharing with teens. Youth may not be prepared to hear us being brutally honest about ourselves.

It is true that the hour spent in Bible study on Sunday morning can be a time of genuine fellowship with teens; but spending time with them away from the church provides the best Christian fellowship—*koinonia.*

The third purpose of Youth Sunday School is to guide youth to fellowship with each other as well as with the entire church.

4. Ministry

Youth today are hurting, and we are more aware of their hurt than ever before. Many of today's teens come from broken or blended homes—where a parent has died or parents are separated by divorce; teens have experienced terminal illness, either personally or with someone who is dear to them; teens live with violence at school; teens see their friends experimenting with drugs and alcohol (and they are experimenting themselves); many teens are contemplating suicide—and the list goes on.

Part of our job as Youth Sunday School leaders is to minister to teens to meet their needs and the needs of their families. A concerned leader provides a listening ear or a shoulder to cry on when necessary. A caring youth leader encourages Christian parents (including single parents) to fulfill their responsibilities as the primary Bible teachers and disciplers of their children. Writing notes of encouragement and concern is part of being a Youth Sunday School leader. Going to ballgames, concerts, plays, track meets, and contests is part of being a Youth Sunday School leader. Visiting the hospital, attending funerals, going to their homes, making phone calls, or eating meals with them at school or after school is part of being a ministering Youth Sunday School leader. Ministry to teens is not just a one-hour-a-week job on Sunday morning. It is almost a full-time job!

The fourth purpose of Youth Sunday School is to minister to teens and their families.

5. Worship

Back in the 1950s and 60s, worship was equated with tradition. In the 1990s worship is often equated with entertainment. Many churches have exciting worship services, and the danger is that the experience might be allowed to take the place of the relationship (with the One to Whom we direct our worship). Sometimes the mindset is such that if the congregation doesn't leave the service with warm, fuzzy feelings, they feel they have not experienced "worship."

Our job is to lead youth to worship both personally and corporately. According to Isaiah 6:1-8, a definition of *worship* could be as follows: *Worship is opening myself up to God so that He can serve me, in order that when I go out into the community I can serve Him.* A personal experience with the Lord or a corporate experience with Him will give God an opportunity to clean us up and make us usable so that when we return to school, work, home, or recreation areas, we can be of service to Him. We honor and glorify Him so that He, the Creator, can work in us and through us to help change the world in which we live. (See chapter 4 for further explanation of personal worship.)

In Youth Sunday School work, remember: If we fail to attend worship and if we fail to participate in worship, we will not be able to guide teens to worship.

The fifth purpose of Youth Sunday School is to guide youth to worship.

The Foundational Strategy

We have defined Sunday School for the 21st century to be the foundational strategy in a local church for leading people to faith in the Lord Jesus Christ and for building Great Commission Christians through Bible study groups that engage people in evangelism, discipleship, fellowship, ministry, and worship. Youth Sunday School is a seven-day-per-week strategy that provides support for all other church ministries. If other church ministries are not present in your church, as the "foundational strategy" Youth Sunday School can provide the foundation to help start one or more additional ministries.

Some examples of how Youth Sunday School relates to other church ministries:

1. *Pastor and other church leadership.*—Youth Sunday School affirms the pastor as the leader in its ministry of building Great Commission Christians. Youth leaders will seek to lead students to worship both personally and corporately, including encouragement to worship through the church's music ministry. With regard to the FAITH Sunday School Evangelism Strategy, the pastor's leadership is essential.

2. *Discipleship.*—Youth Sunday School provides foundational discipleship through Bible teaching for spiritual transformation. Sunday School leaders encourage youth to strengthen their Christian walk by going deeper in other discipleship opportunities. Youth Sunday School leaders help identify discipleship needs of participants. A specific example would be encouraging students involved in the FAITH strategy to move from Student FAITH Basic to Student FAITH Advanced to Student FAITH Discipleship.

→Youth Sunday School is a seven-day-a-week strategy that provides support for all other church ministries.

3. *Family ministry.*—Youth Sunday School operates as a supportive partner with parents, affirming the home as the center of biblical guidance. Youth leaders recognize that parents are to be the primary Bible teachers and disciplers of their youth and encourage families to participate in the church's ministries with families.

4. *Stewardship.*—Youth Sunday School leaders call upon participants to be good stewards, fully involved in the church's overall mission.

5. *Missions.*—Youth Sunday School provides opportunities for youth to be involved in ministry and missions projects as a continuation of Sunday School Bible study. Leaders also prayerfully encourage further involvement in missions through missions organizations and church strategies. Youth classes or departments may designate a ministry team leader to give specific leadership in the church's missions strategies. Leaders will also support giving to support missions.

And the list could go on as long as your church's youth ministry extends! Overall, Sunday School emphasizes ongoing, open Bible study groups that reproduce new groups as the best long-term approach for building a ministry environment that encourages unsaved people to come to faith in Christ, assimilate new believers into the life of the church, and encourages believers to lead others to Christ. Other church ministries then take students deeper into evangelism, discipleship, fellowship, ministry, and worship.

Your Turn . . .

What evidences do you see in your Youth Sunday School that God is at work in evangelism, discipleship, fellowship, ministry, and worship? If you are a new Youth Sunday School leader or aren't sure you see God at work, what do you believe God wants to do through you and your students in the areas of:

•Evangelism____

•Discipleship____

•Fellowship____

•Ministry____

•Worship____

We are motivated because we love God supremely and we want to be obedient.

What Is Our Motivation?

As adults who sense God's leadership to work with youth, we serve these purposes or functions for two basic reasons:

• Because we love God supremely (*The Great Commandment*). Jesus indicated that we are to love God with all our being. We are faithful to evangelize teens, disciple teens, minister to teens, guide teens to fellowship, and guide them to worship because of our great love for the Father (Mark 12:29-30).

• Because we want to be obedient (*The Great Commission*). In the passage that was referred to previously, Jesus did not suggest that we do His work, He commissioned us to do it. The words of His Great Commission were His final remarks to us to ensure that His kingdom continued in His physical absence (Matt. 28:18-20).

At this point, you may be thinking that Youth Sunday School is a big job and you aren't up to the task. Well, you and I are not up to the task; there's no way we can perform all those functions ourselves. But the good news is that we have help through the indwelling presence of the Holy Spirit. Because Jesus lives inside us, He gives us the strength, stamina, and courage to accomplish more with His presence than we could even attempt with our own feeble efforts.

What Could Happen?

This chapter has presented a picture of a purpose-driven™ Youth Sunday School. In Bible study each Sunday (or at any other time!), Youth Sunday School leaders will be evangelizing youth, discipling youth, ministering to youth, fellowshiping with youth, and guiding youth to worship. What greater purpose can we have?

A Youth Sunday School with purpose will have at least four results based on *Kingdom Principles for Church Growth*, by Gene Mims.

Result #1.—Expect numerical growth. As Youth Sunday School leaders and learners perform their functions effectively, one of the results is that more youth will begin to be involved in the Bible Study ministry of your church. Some of them will be Christians, but many of them will not yet have accepted Christ as Savior and Lord. We can rejoice that we will have the opportunity to share with those teens how they, too, can enjoy a personal relationship with the Lord. And for those youth who already are Christians we can share how they can grow as Christians in spiritual maturity.

Result #2.—Expect spiritual growth. A principle that is well worth remembering is this: no amount of doing right things is going to make me a better Christian, but when I do those things I am placed in a growing position so that the Lord can cause me to grow. It is all the Lord. I am only in a growing condition. He produces whatever may be good in my life.

Result #3.—Expect an expansion of the ministries in which we can participate. The stronger the youth of our churches become, the more they will want to reach out to others. Neither they nor we will be satisfied with where we have been before; we will want to reach out beyond ourselves to meet even more needs.

Result #4.—Expect an advancement in our missions awareness and participation. Youth Sunday Schools that participate in the five functions listed above will sense that God is calling them beyond the four walls of their classes and departments to a world that is in need of a personal relationship with the Creator of the Universe. We will not be hoarding our relationship with Him. We will want to be sharing it.

Blessings as you participate in Youth Sunday School with purpose! It is a long, hard process, but the reward of seeing lives changed for eternity is well worth the effort. *Therefore, my dear brothers, stand firm. Let nothing move you. Always give yourselves fully to the work of the Lord, because you know that your labor in the Lord is not in vain* (1 Cor. 15:58, NIV).

The Youth We Teach

Answer the following questions and discover how much you are in touch with youth.

Get In Touch with Today's Youth

1. What songs are currently in the 'Top 40" in any venue (rock, country, rhythm and blues, rap, pop, easy listening)? ______

2. Who are some top recording artists today that are popular with students? ______

3. What movies are playing now that students are viewing? ______

4. How about the top 10 video rentals? ______

5. What are some television shows currently popular among students? ______

6. What magazines do teenage girls read? ______

7. What magazines do teenage boys read? ______

8. What is the most prominent medium of communication in your town right now? ______

9. What would you guess is the average amount of money spent each week by a teenager in the United States? ______

10. In your opinion, what is the greatest difficulty with which students have to deal today? ______

If you are like most folks who relate to teenagers, you might sometimes say, "I don't need to be working with youth because I'm just not in touch with them." Believe it or not, you are not alone—most adults are not in touch with the culture in which students are living today. Those of us who work with teens, however, do need to make an effort to get in touch—not only with their culture, but also with what is going on with their minds and bodies during these important growing-up years.

The goal of this chapter is to help you get started on the constant journey of staying in touch with students' culture, developmental issues, and generational characteristics.

→Don't get too proud about knowing what the "Top 40" songs are this week because they will change next week.

Youth Culture

The answers to most of the preceding questions can be found in local newspapers or magazines. Staying in touch may simply mean that you know where to find the information. (But don't feel too proud of yourself for knowing what the "Top 40" songs are this week; they will surely change next week!) A list of top recording artists also changes frequently. Very few musicians enjoy longevity on the popularity lists of students today. All they have to do is release a bad song and they could be "sent packing" in the minds of students.

The world of TV, movies and videos is different. There are some movies popular among students today that were released a dozen or more years ago. Be aware that most city newspapers have an entertainment section (usually on Friday or Saturday) that contains a synopsis of all movies that are currently playing. What this means for you as a youth worker is that you don't have to go to the movie to find out what it's about—you can read about it. Also, there are entertainment magazines that give reviews that are helpful to you. Here's the point: As parents and youth leaders, we do not want to encourage students to watch some of the current movies, but we know they are watching them anyway. What we are looking for is a teachable moment on Sunday or during the week that will drive home a spiritual truth. So, if we quote a line from a current movie or make reference to a character in that movie, or show a video clip, for that moment we have the attention of the students in our class and we can make the biblical point we desire to make without necessarily endorsing the movie.

Remember the strategic principles referred to in the Introduction? Staying in touch with youth culture relates to the principles of family responsibility, spiritual transformation, and biblical leadership and the related best practice of teaching to transform.

3 Family Responsibility

4 Spiritual Transformation

5 Biblical Leadership

You can go to the music store in your mall and find out the "Top 10" songs in any venue. In the same newspaper entertainment section mentioned above, you can find the "Top 40" songs for the week. In the church I attend, I was the eighth-grade department director a few years ago. One Sunday morning we were listing some things on a large sheet of paper during our department time, and in the course of the listing I happened to mention the name of a guitarist in a popular band. You would not believe the incredulous looks I received from those eighth graders. "You know the name of the guitarist from _________?" (I don't even remember the name of the

Spiritual Transformation 4

band or guitarist now!) The point is that for that one moment I had them. It was the teachable moment I desired, and I was able to drive home the point of the lesson because I happened to mention some guy I didn't know or listen to. As youth leaders we need to remember that their culture is important to teenagers, and when we know something about it, we can teach them what they *need* to know.

Pick up a couple of teen magazines and glance through them.

Magazines are another avenue through which teens are influenced by their culture. Remember, too, that if a magazine is intended for a specific age, it's a pretty sure thing students who are two or three years younger than that age are reading it. Older teenage girls read a lot of adult magazines. It's not always necessary to purchase all of these magazines to know what your youth are reading. As you stand in line at the grocery store, pick up a couple of the magazines and glance through them—you'll get a pretty good idea of what is influencing teenage girls. Specifically, look at the ads and the question-and-answer articles. You will probably find that there are many things in those magazines that do not reflect Christian values and that will upset you as a Youth Sunday School leader.

Guys, on the other hand, do not read text closely—they mostly look through the magazines. Pick up some magazines for guys and peruse them—you'll find articles and ads for sports, fashion, vehicles, wrestling, bodybuilding, hunting, fishing, and music. As you seek to teach teens the truths of the Scripture, it is important to be aware of the tremendous influence this medium has on their lives!

Radio and television are, as we all know, the most influential media in the lives of teenagers. Although many students are spending more and more time on the Internet, they also listen to 28-30 hours a week of professionally recorded music on the radio or their stereos. And they spend that many hours watching TV each week. Add up those hours—it is staggering to think about what is going into their minds that is influencing them as they grow up! The statistics for the amount of violence, inappropriate sexual behavior, and profanity that is being viewed and listened to are almost more than we can comprehend. Considering that we teachers have only 45-60 minutes in each Bible study session, it's obvious that we have our work cut out for us! And the time element places even more importance on seven-day-a-week teaching and ministering.

It's no news to you that materialism is rampant in our country, and students are caught up in it just as we adults are. Our young people control an enormous amount of money. In the United States, students between the ages of 12 and 20 spend an amount that is equal to half of the national defense budget for this country! In 1998, that was $100 billion annually—spent on cars, clothes, gasoline, insurance, videos, and compact disks. In order to spend that kind of money, most youth must have a job. Many of your older students work 15 to 25 hours a week in addition to the other extracurricular activities that demand their time and attention.

5 Biblical Leadership

Finally, the difficulties related to the youth culture are many. Peer pressure, integrity, cheating, drugs, alcohol, tobacco, premarital sexual activity, family problems, and violence are some of the problems most of today's teens will have to face. Overriding all of those struggles, however, is the issue of self-image. If a student feels pretty good about himself or herself, he or she is less likely to participate in self-destructive behavior. The problem is that even students who have everything going for them often have difficulty feeling good about themselves. Remembering this, we adults who work with youth must be aware that it is never appropriate for us to cut down a student—even as a joke. We should always look for ways to affirm them and build them up so they have an idea of who they are in Christ. This does not mean we can't correct them; it means that we will not be negative or tolerate them being cutting with each other.

So, it's obvious their culture is a tremendous influence in the lives of students. As you and I seek to teach them the Scripture, we will be well served by being sensitive to what is going on in their changing culture.

Developmental Life Issues

In the United States by the year 2005, there will be over 30 million teenagers. Much of the growth will be in ethnic (African, Asian, and Hispanic American) populations. Research indicates that by the middle of the first decade of the twenty-first century, there will be more teenagers in the United States than ever before, including the Baby Boomers' youth years. Most sociologists agree that although the present generation of youth known as Millennials or PowerBuilders (born from about 1980-2000) has many positive characteristics, it is also a generation that is in trouble. Many of these same sociologists also say that this generation is very open and sensitive to spiritual issues. That makes PowerBuilders, the most unreached generation in history, also the most reachable generation in history. Perhaps the struggles and difficulties that have made them unreachable have also made them the most open to the gospel of Jesus Christ.

→PowerBuilders (Millennials) are the most reachable generation in history.

If churches are to be successful at impacting the youth of their communities they are going to have to be creative and passionate about taking the gospel of Christ to those youth. Youth ministers and workers must invest in the lives of teenagers at their points of need or risk missing the opportunity to impact them with the gospel forever and thus lose a generation ripe for the Kingdom of God.

Teenagers can be taught, equipped, and involved in the work of ministry and impacting their generation for Christ. They can take positions of leadership and be held accountable for their actions. They can understand, with growing awareness, the deep mysteries of the faith. But they are adolescents, and those that minister to youth must consider their developmental maturity (or lack of) and minister to them with loving care and nurture. (Not an easy task sometimes!)

2 Foundational Discipleship

Once when I was enlisting workers to teach seventh graders, I approached a lady who was very gifted and seemed to be a likely candidate to work with that age group. I asked her to consider that teaching position, and her answer still sticks with me—after almost 20 years: "I don't have to pray about that one; the answer is NO!" As I have reflected on that lady's response, I realized her immediate reaction was not due to spiritual insensitivity, it was her "teenage developmental insensitivity." She probably didn't understand seventh graders, so she wouldn't even consider working with them! It's certainly true that not everyone is cut out to be a middle school worker; but sometimes there are folks who would make great middle school workers if they knew what was going on in the lives of those seventh and eighth graders—and knew what to expect from them.

To be sure, the physical changes a teenager experiences are complex. There are also other dimensions of a teenager's development that those who minister to them need to understand. It is important to study and learn about how youth are developing, not only physically, but intellectually, emotionally, socially, and spiritually as well. Remember, the characteristics mentioned here are general; in your youth group there will be exceptions to each of these descriptions.

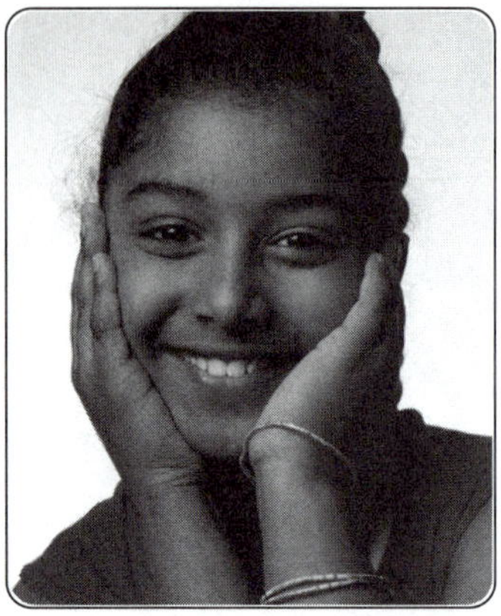

→ Younger youth are usually most comfortable in same-sex groups.

Younger Youth (12-15 years old)

1. Physical Development
   - At the onset of puberty, a youth looks very much like a child.
   - Puberty puts the body in rapid overdrive. Hormones kick in, causing massive growth spurts and the initiationof the sex drive causes all kinds of physical changes. Secondary sexual characteristics are developing.
   - Weight fluctuates; girls are especially conscious of this change. Guys and girls are awkward because of these growth spurts.
   - Acne may become a problem for many youth and it can affect their self-esteem and emotional development in a number of ways.
2. Emotional Development
   - They begin to develop their own sense of identity.
   - They are self-conscious and self-centered, but are gaining self-confidence.
   - They are full of enthusiasm.
   - They'd love to be independent, but are still dependent on their parents.
   - They vacillate between being friendly and being moody.
3. Social Development
   - They want to fit in. High value is placed on same-sex relationships.
   - They are often cliquish; they have a few close friends.
   - They are often overly critical and have unrealistic expectations of themselves and others.
   - Guys start getting interested in girls (girls have already developed interest in the opposite sex).
   - Hero worship and crushes are common.
   - They are usually most comfortable in same-sex groups.
   - They test the limits and experiment with different behaviors.
4. Mental Development
   - They don't necessarily accept others' beliefs (especially their parents'). They want proof.
   - At about age 12, youth move into the early stages of abstract thinking and what is called the formal operations stage. They can begin to understand abstract concepts such as social justice and rational, aesthetic, or social ideals.
   - They enjoy problem solving, looking for alternatives and consequences.
   - Personal values are beginning to influence their decisions.
   - Early on in this process, adolescents tend to be very clumsy in their decision making. They begin to think of so many alternatives that they make poor decisions.
5. Spiritual Development
   - The very first step in the spiritual life is for the person to know he or she is loved—based simply on being, with no regard to performance or accomplishment.
   - They are generally interested in a relationship with Christ. (Up to 80 percent of people make professions of faith before they are 18.)
   - They are able to make genuine commitments, although these commitments may have to be revisited as they grow older.
   - Right and wrong are prominent in their thinking.
   - Initially, this group tends to mirror its parents' personal values.
   - They can respond to social issues and have a great ability to respond to the needs of those who are less fortunate than they.

Older Youth (16-18 years old)

1. Physical Development
    - By the end of puberty, youth look very much like adults.
    - Until about age 16, girls precede boys in physical development by about two years, and are far ahead of their male peers in emotional maturity.
    - They are very interested in personal health.
    - They have tendencies toward eating disorders (especially girls).
    - Many are sexually experienced.
    - Acne is a problem for many youth and it can affect their self-esteem and emotional development.
2. Emotional Development
    - They are fairly confident and secure with their own identity.
    - They seek deeper, more meaningful relationships than before.
    - They possess a desire for independence.
    - They are aware of the need to be responsible for their own actions.
    - They tend to be friendly toward their family.
    - They are more giving of themselves; there is less self-centeredness.
3. Social Development
    - They desire meaningful relationships, especially with members of the opposite sex.
    - They are frequent daters.
    - Their personal relationships tend to be more exclusive, especially in their relationships with members of the opposite sex.
    - Many are sexually active.
    - They have experienced rites of passage—getting a driver's license and upcoming graduation from high school.
    - Most of them work part-time, which means they have spending money.
4. Mental Development
    - They are very interested in the future.
    - They have begun to focus on their careers.
    - They recognize that decisions they make today affect their futures.
    - They have the ability to process many things at one time.
    - They tend to make better and more mature decisions than younger youth.
    - They have the ability to resolve conflicts maturely.
    - They learn to think more multidimensionally rather than being limited to single issues.
5. Spiritual Development
    - They show the ability to make and keep a strong commitment to Christ.
    - Their moral and spiritual values are often challenged at school and in social relationships.
    - They are very interested in life after death.
    - They are no longer content to believe what parents, ministers, and leaders have taught them up to this point. They want to understand and decide for themselves what they believe and why.
    - They have the ability to grasp and apply deeper spiritual principles to their own lives than younger youth.
    - An important evolution takes place as teenagers transition through adolescence. It is a radical redirection from a "received faith" to an "owned faith." "Received Faith" is that faith obtained through the environment

Older youth are very interested in personal health.

and culture where a teenager lives (family and community). "Owned faith" happens when teenagers take on the responsibility for their own beliefs, actions, and lifestyles.

Sixth Grade—An Important Transition

A question frequently asked by youth ministers is, "Where should we put sixth graders for Bible study, and what materials are best to use with them?" Ultimately, each church has to make its own decision on that subject, but I recommend sixth graders remain in the Children's ministry area of church. If yours is a small church, you may want to start a preteen ministry for fifth and sixth graders. If you are ministering in a larger church, a separate sixth-grade ministry may be the best option for you.

Consider these things as you seek to do the very best for the sixth graders in your care.

1. Sixth graders may be in middle school in your local school system, but that doesn't mean your church has to comply with that organization. Please make your decisions based on what is best for the sixth graders in your church.

2. Remember that whether sixth graders are in middle school or in elementary school, they will still learn at a sixth-grade level developmentally. Sixth graders tend to think and learn in concrete ways, so their curriculum and learning environment need to be designed to meet those needs.

3. Most sixth graders are not anywhere near teenagers developmentally, especially in the social realm. Although some sixth grade girls may be physically mature, their social skills are not up to the level of older teens. Putting a physically mature sixth-grade girl in close proximity with a tenth-grade boy has disaster written all over it.

4. Self-esteem is another factor to be considered in the decision of where to place sixth graders. These students may only be two years behind the other youth chronologically, but they are farther behind socially and emotionally. Great care must be taken to keep situations from developing where a sixth grader cannot compete on the same skill level as older youth. Early failure can result in feelings of poor self-esteem.

5. Many youth ministers want to include sixth graders in order to increase the size of their youth groups, but in many cases older teenagers stop coming to the youth activities when sixth graders are present because they aren't willing to be patient with the less mature social skills of the younger students.

6. There is something to be said for having to wait for some things in life. Often sixth graders experience what all other youth are experiencing and when they are older they suffer from boredom—and even drop out of participation.

Make your decisions about sixth grade based on what is best for the children in your church.

The important thing, of course, is to help your sixth graders have the best possible church experience. If you already have sixth graders in your ministry or if space or numbers dictate that you must have them in your youth ministry, please make every effort to assure that they have the opportunity to learn and mature at their own level. It is difficult at best, and requires hard and consistent work. If you need more information about this particular aspect of student ministry, refer to *Children's Sunday School for A New Century* by James Hargrave (available at LifeWay Christian Stores).

12th Grade–Another Important Transition

Special attention should also be given to the needs of high school seniors. The final year in high school is a time of transition and preparation. Ideally, 12th graders need a class specifically designed to address their concerns about preparing to leave home and be on their own in a world of checkbooks, dirty laundry, academic responsibility, faith questions, new friends, and so on. LifeWay provides a topical Bible study especially for seniors during their last quarter in Youth Sunday School. This study is ideal for the spring quarter leading up to a special Senior Day celebration in your church.

Some churches promote seniors into the college department shortly after their graduation. This provides seniors the chance to be involved with youth and college students during the summer after graduation. Whatever you choose to do, remember that this group of teenagers has unique needs.

Generational Life Issues

By the year 2005 there will be over 30 million teenagers in the United States, with many of them being in ethnic populations (African, Asian, and Hispanic American). As you prepare to teach and minister to this group of students, it is helpful to consider their generational characteristics. There will probably be no members of Generation X or the Boomer Generation in your youth ministry–unless they are some of your leaders.

The generation of students to which this book is directed is the Millennial Generation, or PowerBuilders. They are youth whose birth years are between 1982 and 2000. This generation represents the last high school graduating class of this century. The first of this group will graduate in the year 2000 and the rest will take us into the 21st century. Their membership is still growing, and most of this generation could live past America's Tricentennial in 2076!

Many sociologists have called these millennials the next "good" generation. They seem to embody the best of the two previous generations. It looks like they will be conservative, civic-minded, cooperative, and have more tendencies toward religion than previous generations. Health care, family, and education are high priorities for this generation. PowerBuilders will grow up in a world stressing more values, more structure, and more protection. George Barna says that they describe themselves as serious, stressed out, self-reliant, skeptical, survivors, and spiritual.[1]

How does this information relate to us as youth workers? It helps prepare us to minister to them. Though much of the generational information relates to their culture, much also relates to who they have become and who they are becoming in response to what previous generations have experienced. An online survey of nearly 17,000 folks between the ages of 15 and 24 rendered the following responses. (If you are sharp you will easily be able to discern the information that comes from the older respondents to this survey.) Obviously, some of these topics are outdated for younger youth, but the point of sharing this information is to let you know how many of this generation are thinking. Some of it is encouraging. Much of it is challenging, as we think about how to best meet their needs.

→The generation of students to which this book is directed is the Millennial Generation or PowerBuilders. Many have called this generation the next "good" generation.

The Defining Moments of This Generation

1. Challenger Explosion
2. The Fall of the Berlin Wall
3. Rise of the Internet
4. The Gulf War
5. Oklahoma City Bombing
6. Introduction of the Nintendo Entertainment System
7. The death of Princess Diana
8. L.A. Riots
9. O.J.'s slow-speed Bronco chase
10. Re-release of *Star Wars*
11. Launch of MTV
12. Kurt Cobain found dead
13. Waco Siege (tie)
14. Tiananmen Square Massacre (tie)
15. Release of the movie *Titanic*

The Heroes of this Generation

1. Luke Skywalker (attributed to the re-release of *Star Wars)*
2. Jesus Christ
3. Michael Jordan
4. Martin Luther King
5. Our parents
6. Mother Teresa
7. Princess Diana
8. Steven Spielberg
9. The man in front of the tank (from Tiananmen Square)
10. Bill Gates
11. Howard Stern
12. Dilbert (tie)
12. Jerry Springer (tie)

Most Important TV Shows of This Generation

1. The Simpsons
2. Seinfeld
3. The X-Files
4. South Park
5. The Late Show with David Letterman
6. Married with Children
7. Saturday Night Live
8. The Jerry Springer Show
9. Star Trek: Next Generation
10. ER

The Villains of this Generation

1. Saddam Hussein
2. Barney
3. O.J. Simpson
4. The Internal Revenue Service
5. Satan
6. Bill Clinton
7. Bill Gates
8. Timothy McVeigh
9. Unabomber
10. Darth Vader
11. Jeffrey Dahmer
12. Charles Manson
13. Michael Jackson

Most Important Movies of This Generation

1. Star Wars
2. Braveheart
3. The Empire Strikes Back
4. Pulp Fiction
5. Return of the Jedi
6. Titanic
7. T2: Judgment Day
8. Schindler's List (tie)
8. Ferris Bueller's Day Off (tie)
10. Scream
11. Raiders of the Lost Ark
12. Aliens
13. Die Hard
14. Breakfast Club
15. The Princess Bride

Most Important Albums of this Generation

1. Nirvana: Nevermind
2. Metallica: Master of Puppets
3. Nine Inch Nails: The Downward Spiral
4. Pearl Jam: 10
5. U2: The Joshua Tree
6. Pink Floyd: The Wall
7. Guns 'n' Roses: Appetite for Destruction
8. Smashing Pumpkins: Siamese Dream
9. Alanis Morrissette: Jagged Little Pill
10. Notorious B.I.G.: Life After Death

Most Important Computer and Video Games for this Generation

1. Zelda Series
2. Final Fantasy Series
3. Resident Evil/Resident Evil 2
4. Quake/Quake 2
5. Tomb Raider/Tomb Raider 2
6. Super Mario 64
7. Doom Series
8. Golden Eye
9. Tetris (tie)
10. Street Fighter Series (tie)

Our Clothing

1. Nike
2. Levi's
3. Tommy Hilfiger
4. Adidas
5. Calvin Klein
6. The Gap
7. Doc Marten
8. Polo/Ralph Lauren
9. Old Navy
10. Eddie Bauer

Our Drinks

1. Coca-Cola
2. Mountain Dew
3. Pepsi
4. Water
5. Dr. Pepper

(Copyright 1998 Image Media)

Regardless of your personal feelings about culture, developmental processes, and generational thinking, these things are affecting the lives of the students to whom we are trying to make known the claims of Christ. We are not in this process alone. God's Holy Spirit is helping us make a difference in the lives of students all over the world. Depend on Him as you seek to meet their needs.

[1] Barna, George. *Generation Next; What You need to Know About Today's Youth,* Ventura, California, Regal Books, 1995.

Chapter 3

The Process of Youth Sunday School:

Identify the Strategy and Organize with Purpose

We have probably all had experience with "Traffic Light" Sunday School teachers—they are the people who pray for red lights on the way to church so they can study their lesson for that day. It sounds ludicrous, but the scenario is similar to that of many workers preparing for Sunday morning Bible study with youth.

I believe we would all agree that this is not the ideal way to teach Youth Sunday School. For an effective Bible study session to take place there needs to be study and planning. Planning should be a priority; planning is necessary; and planning is biblical—"For I know the plans I have for you," declares the Lord, "plans to prosper you and not to harm you, plans to give you hope and a future," (Jer. 29:11). God has a plan for our lives, and whether we follow it or not, His plan is in place.

As Youth Sunday School workers, we are seeking change. We desire to see teenagers who don't know Christ brought to faith in Him, and those who know Christ brought to maturity through spiritual transformation. We cannot lead youth to change until we develop plans that make the best use of resources (including people) to implement constructive and committed change. "Do your best to present yourself to God as one approved, a workman who does not need to be ashamed and who correctly handles the word of truth" (2 Tim. 2:15).

Prepare

What should be included in the process of doing Youth Sunday School? The first thing is preparation. That is an all-inclusive word, and one ingredient is the fact that we Youth Sunday School leaders must be prepared spiritually. An important observation about being spiritually prepared is a common phrase—"More is caught than taught" when it comes to working with teens. If we are growing spiritually, then it will be evident to the teens we teach each week, and they will learn by our example. The leader is the lesson!

Biblical Leadership 5

→The leader is the lesson!

Another part of preparation is the preparation for the lesson itself. It's not enough to be spiritually prepared—we also need to have a well-thought out Bible study lesson ready on Sunday morning. Here is a good agenda to get prepared for the lesson each week:

1. Sunday afternoon (before the next week's lesson):
    - Read the Scripture passages for this week's session.
    - Pray for class members' needs, in light of the Bible passage.
    - Determine how this lesson fits into the unit and how it relates to last week's lesson.

2. Monday:
    - Read the Scripture passages again and the commentary portion of the leader guide.
    - Review last Sunday's plan and evaluate it in light of how the students responded to the session. What were the strong and weak points of the session? Did the youth respond to the teaching procedures used?
    - Pray for each youth by name.

3. Tuesday:
    - Begin to make notes on the plan sheet. (See Appendix.)
    - Check the kit items and the learner guide to see how they fit into the teaching plan.
    - Spend time studying the Scripture passage, and pray for insight and understanding.
    - Select a key verse to memorize or begin memorizing the Memory Verse for that session.

4. Wednesday:
    - Attend weekly leadership meeting, and complete the plan sheet (If your planning meeting is on a different night, adjust as necessary).
    - Discuss the procedures for Sunday morning, and share thoughts about the meaning of the Scripture passage(s).
    - Continue memorizing the Memory Verse.
    - Share with the other workers prayer requests for the known needs of your youth and how the lesson can relate to them.

5. Thursday:
    - Choose a key word from the lesson.
    - Do a verse search on the key word, using a concordance.
    - Read the Bible passage once more, and make necessary changes to the plan sheet.
    - Pray for your youth.

6. Friday:
    - Gather all resource materials needed for Sunday morning; be sure you understand how to use them.
    - Pray for the Holy Spirit to guide the Sunday morning session.

7. Saturday:
    - Mentally walk through your plans for Sunday morning.
    - Look over the lesson as a whole, making sure the different parts that have been worked on during the week flow together.
    - Pray once again for each youth and each known need.

4 Spiritual Transformation

5 Biblical Leadership

You may need to adjust these actions to fit your time schedule, but this is a good weekly plan for getting yourself ready to teach the lesson.

No one ever said planning is easy. Planning takes time, effort, and commitment.

Biblical Leadership 5

Plan

The second step in the process of doing Youth Sunday School was referenced under the Wednesday activities in the preceding outline—the need for youth workers to plan together as a team. The most effective planning is done weekly. Occasionally, workers may plan a unit at a time, meeting monthly. Remember that this planning requires three or four hours to prepare a basic procedure for each week of the month. The department director will need to call workers each week to confirm final arrangements.

In addition to weekly and monthly planning, annual planning is important. Annual planning includes evaluating the past year's accomplishments, determining goals for the new Sunday School year, evaluating space and equipment, planning and conducting worker training, and developing class and department organization. For more detailed information on planning, see *Sunday School for A New Century,* by Bill L. Taylor and Louis B. Hanks.

No one ever said planning is easy. Planning takes time, effort, and commitment. Even if you are the only youth worker, you are not the only person who will be planning for Sunday School. If possible, plan with other teachers from your church. For more detail on planning for Youth Sunday School, see chapter 5.

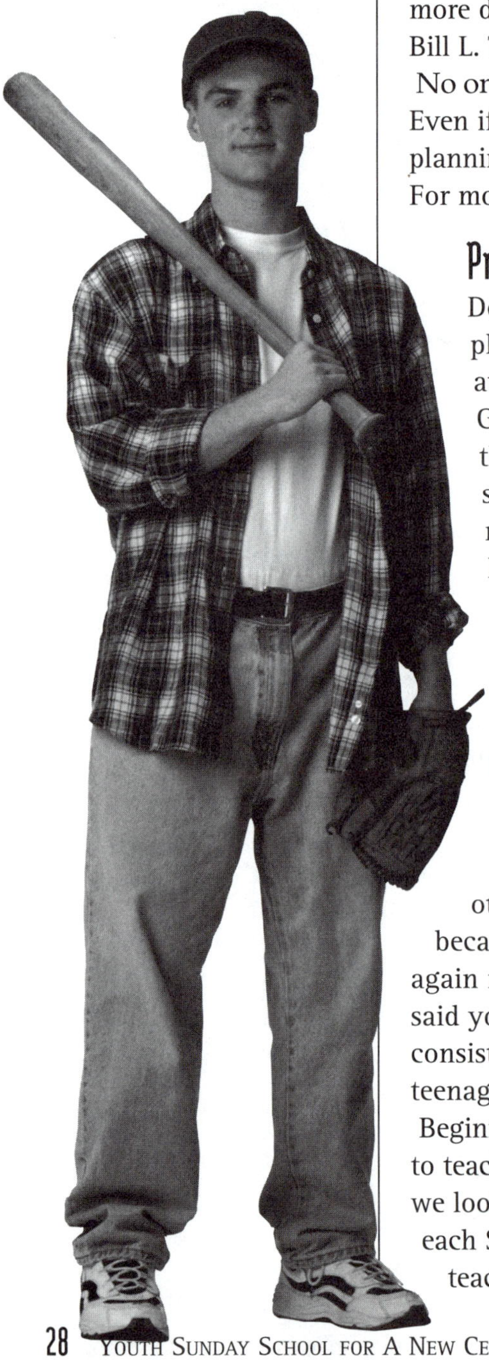

Practice

Do you recognize the name of Tony Gwynn? He is a professional baseball player, and the first major league player since Ted Williams to have a chance at a season batting average of .400. In the strike-shortened season in 1994, Gwynn was flirting with that .400 average. In addition to that, Tony is one of the finest hitters in major league history, having hit over .300 nearly every season he has been in the major leagues. Stop and think about this fact for a moment: Tony Gwynn makes millions of dollars each year for getting a hit less than 40% of the time!

Now, how does that story apply to Youth Sunday School workers? The point is that no one—not even a successful person—bats 1.000. We can't allow ourselves to be discouraged when what we plan and try to do with our teenagers is not successful 100% of the time. We must continue practicing good Youth Sunday School principles. Instead of giving up on a teaching method when it doesn't work as you think it should, practice doing it again—maybe in a little different way; instead of giving up on a teenager who doesn't seem to respond to your contacts and your concern, practice other ways of demonstrating that you care; instead of giving up on planning because the meeting didn't turn out exactly like you wanted, practice doing it again next week. You get the point—Youth Sunday School takes practice. No one said youth work is easy, and a successful outcome is based on commitment and consistency. It takes long, hard, enduring practice to make sure that the lives of teenagers have an opportunity to be changed.

Beginning in the fall of 2000, LifeWay curriculum will incorporate a new approach to teaching, using the terms *Prepare, Encounter,* and *Continue.* Earlier in this chapter we looked at the preparation part. To have a quality Youth Sunday School lesson each Sunday requires that you prepare yourself spiritually and that you prepare to teach the lesson. Additionally, you will need to plan with your team so that the specific Bible Study experience comes off in a way to transform the lives of teenagers. *Prepare* includes the motivation part of the session.

Biblical Leadership 5 The *Encounter* part of the session refers to the Bible study experience itself. Most youth do not come to Bible study all fired up to study the Bible. In fact, since most of them do not even bring their Bibles, the first thing we must do in our session is to "hook" them into the study. The first step in the teaching plan will always be designed to create a desire for Bible study in the hearts and minds of the youth who are present on Sunday morning. The final part of the *Encounter* section seeks to apply the meaning of the Scripture to a person's daily life. The final step of learning must be application. What we learn about God in Bible study must be put into practice in our individual lives. As youth workers, our job in Youth Sunday School is to help youth determine a plan of action for what they will do with the insights from their study. This may be the most difficult part of the session. If transformation is to take place in the lives of the youth we teach, they must utilize what they have learned.

Spiritual Transformation 4 Transformational Bible study cannot take place by simply examining Scripture for one hour each week—scriptural truths must be applied every day of the week. So, the most meaningful Bible Study begins with the Sunday morning experience and continues throughout the week. This final element of *Encounter* is also the beginning of the *Continue* part of the study. In chapter 1 we introduced as one of the strategic principles for Youth Sunday School the seven-day Bible study experience. It's true that this philosophy puts an enormous amount of responsibility on the youth leader, because now that person must not only get ready for Sunday, he or she must follow up on the lives of each of his or her students to make sure they are putting into practice what they have learned. In addition to the teacher, however, the materials will also guide youth to put the Scripture into practice each day of the week. More detailed information about *Prepare*, *Encounter*, and *Continue* is found in chapter 6.

The first three steps in the Youth Sunday School process are *Preparation*, *Planning*, and *Practice*. The final step in this process is one with which you are well acquainted; it is vital to the success of Youth Sunday School—*Prayer*.

. . . And Pray!

As Youth Sunday School leaders we need to communicate with God about everything related to the Bible study experience, including the youth we teach, the team with whom we work, the materials we use to study His Word, and the context of our study—the church.

In the section above that talked about getting ready for the lesson, one thing came through loud and clear. We must pray for the youth we teach. If we desire transformational Bible study, we must be aware of the needs of our youth and take those to the Father for His care. One of the things I have learned through years as a youth minister is that youth like to know that a person is praying for them. All of us like to hear our names mentioned out loud to God in prayer—youth are no different. Tell youth you are praying for them. They will appreciate it, and they may let you in on some secrets for prayer that no one else knows.

However, we can't just pray for the youth—our team needs prayer also. We need to mention to God the needs of our fellow team members in Youth Sunday School.

Most youth do not come to Bible study all fired up to study the Bible.

Praying for the unity of your Youth Sunday School team is important.

Praying for the unity of the team is important, as well as praying that we will be able to share the insight necessary for life-changing Bible study. It is quite appropriate to pray about the choice of resources to be used in addition to praying about how we will use them. God can use us in many ways if we are willing to be used.

Bible study is not done in a vacuum. It takes place in the context of the local body of believers that meet at your church's address. It is important for your teaching team and for your youth to make a habit of praying for your pastor, your staff, other age groups, and the needs of your church. Don't neglect any of these in your prayer life.

First Thessalonians 5:17 is an interesting verse. In some translations it says, "Pray without ceasing." In others it states, "Pray continually." The Greek translation actually indicates even more than that–the word for pray is in the present imperative tense in Greek. It could be literally translated, "Keep on praying without ceasing." For emphasis, Paul calls us to never stop praying. If Youth Sunday School is going to provide the opportunity for students' lives to be transformed, it will require of the leaders that they be in a constant state of communication with the Heavenly Father. He cares infinitely more about the spiritual needs of the youth we teach than we do. Let's keep on praying without ceasing. It will make a difference!

Remember Tony Gwynn? He was committed to being a great hitter. As Youth Sunday School workers we are making a commitment to be great teachers.

Organizing for Youth Sunday School

Biblical Leadership 5

Organization is a tool by which leaders and learners are engaged in the strategic areas of the work of the church and Sunday School. Youth Sunday School organization does much more than bring structure–it provides a way to meet the needs of youth, and fulfill our God-given purpose.

The Youth Sunday School Division is designed for youth ages 12-17 or in grades 7-12. Classes may include boys' classes, girls' classes, and/or coed classes. Youth may be grouped according to age, school grade, age segments (older/younger), or gender.

The small group, or class, is the basic unit of Youth Sunday School. The class leadership team usually consists of a teacher and one or more class leaders. Youth class leaders may be enlisted for months or quarters; six months is usually the maximum length of service. Some classes may choose to have an outreach-evangelism leader, but in most Youth Sunday Schools the outreach-evangelism leader functions on a department level. (Detailed job descriptions are found in the appendix.) In medium and large churches, the maximum class enrollment should be 12. There should be one teacher for up to 12 youth enrolled. As enrollment increases, new classes should be created.

For smaller churches, it may be necessary to group all youth together. Whenever possible, at least two classes should be provided, one for older youth and one for younger. It is difficult to effectively teach to meet the needs of youth in a class with 7th to 12th graders all together.

Class Structure and Class Leaders

Class organization can be shaped in many ways, based on how teachers and class leaders approach leadership and share duties with one another and with members. A class leader is enlisted by the teacher to assist with the total work of the class in one or more of the following five areas of work. The five key areas of Sunday School work include:

Foundational Evangelism 1

Evangelism.–Leaders create an atmosphere that encourages unsaved youth to place their faith in Jesus Christ and encourage believers to lead others to Christ. In churches participating in the Student FAITH Sunday School evangelism strategy, members of this leadership team also should be on Student FAITH teams.

Discipleship.—Leaders create an atmosphere that encourages believers to grow in maturity in Christ; monitors the discipleship needs of believers; and works with a church's Discipleship director to provide learning opportunities for youth that help them grow toward spiritual maturity.

Fellowship.—Leaders create an atmosphere conducive to members building relationships with one another as together they build on their relationships with God; lead actions that help new members be assimilated into the fellowship of the class and the team or group to which they are assigned.

Ministry.—Leaders create an atmosphere in which members and prospects can experience direct care and concern for life's needs and avenues through which they may identify and implement missions projects and missions efforts that make the best use of their gifts and abilities. Leaders also lead out in intercessory prayer as an integral part of the ministry and missionary efforts of the class.

Worship.—Leaders create a worshipful atmosphere, lead small-group worship experiences, and encourage members and prospects to develop and participate in personal and family worship experiences in their homes.

Two basic approaches to class organization are: (1) a leader-based approach; or (2) a team-based approach.

The Leader-based Approach

The leader-based approach calls for leaders who accept a position of leadership and assume responsibility for that area of work for the class. Class leaders are needed for the areas of evangelism, discipleship, fellowship, ministry, and worship. (In smaller classes one person may lead more than one responsibility area, such as evangelism-fellowship or discipleship-worship.) Small groups of up to six members and prospects can be assigned to each ministry leader. As needed, a class coordinator can be enlisted to relieve the teacher of administrative responsibilities and to work with both the teacher and class leaders to ensure that the class is fulfilling its responsibilities in the five key areas. This organization assumes that one individual leader is responsible for the assignment rather than a team of people who accept that same assignment.

2 Foundational Discipleship

→Two basic approaches to class organization are leader-based and team-based.

The Team-Based Approach

The team-based approach is built around teams of leaders who share responsibility for engaging people in the class in a specific area of work. Leaders are needed for five teams: evangelism team, discipleship team, fellowship team, ministry team, and worship team. Members and prospects are encouraged to commit to participate in one of the five teams. Leaders for each team can be chosen by the teacher or by the team itself. If there are class members who are involved in Student FAITH, those individuals are the logical ones to lead the evangelism team. Team members share responsibilities with the team leader for meeting specific needs for the entire class in the team's assigned area. As needed, a class coordinator can be enlisted to relieve the teacher of administrative responsibilities

1 Foundational Evangelism

Class members involved in Student FAITH should lead the evangelism team.

and to work with both the teacher and class leaders to ensure that the class is fulfilling its responsibilities in the five key areas.

The team-based approach can also be dealt with comprehensively. The class would be divided into teams of up to six members and prospects. Each team would engage in all five of the key areas—evangelism, discipleship, fellowship, ministry, and worship—for that team only. The outreach-evangelism leader would coordinate work with all of the teams related to evangelism. A class coordinator can be added to evaluate whether all needs are being met.

Departments

In an organization with two or more classes, a department should be created. Department enrollment should not exceed 60 youth; department groupings are usually based on age or grade in school. The department leadership team consists of a department director, a department outreach-evangelism leader, department secretary, and teachers. (Job descriptions are found in the appendix.) If the church is a FAITH church, the department outreach-evangelism leader may also function as the Student FAITH team leader.

There may be some youth with special learning needs that require extra attention when designing the Youth Sunday School organization. In some churches youth with special needs may be grouped in a special education unit; others may be mainstreamed into existing departments and classes. Mainstreaming youth with mental retardation can be difficult without a positive, receptive leader, sensitized peers, and an additional helper for a period of adjustment. Youth can appreciate "being different" and can more easily accept differences of abilities in other youth if there is appropriate sensitizing.

4 Spiritual Transformation

Consider these examples: Youth with hearing impairments may require a special grouping, but they may also be grouped with their peers if they are proficient at lip reading or signing. Youth with visual impairments can be grouped with their peers, but the teacher and others need to be sensitive to their visual limitations. People who speak a language other than that which is dominant in the church may require a special group taught in their language. The point is, when a youth's needs require special groupings every effort should be made to provide those groups. See *Sunday School for A New Century* for additional information on Sunday School ministry for persons with special needs.

4 Spiritual Transformation

When Should We Start a New Class/Department?

As a general rule, consider creating a new unit when:

- All youth are in one class or department;
- More than 12 youth are enrolled in a class;
- More than 60 youth are enrolled in one department;
- A class or department has less than 50 percent enrollment in attendance;
- A school grade has more prospects than youth enrolled.

New youth classes can be started at any time, but the start of the new church year and midyear are ideal times for starting new classes. New classes should be started with under six youth enrolled, thus allowing for growth in the class. As classes and departments grow, creating new units becomes a priority for at least two important reasons:

1. Youth need the experience of large and small groups. Normally, in the small-group setting, youth become personally involved, sharing their feelings and asking tough questions. Creating new classes and departments allows for this personal involvement, and it keeps the focus on meeting the needs of youth.

Spiritual Transformation 4

2. When new units are created, the leadership team expands and the load of responsibility is shared among more people. New classes and departments grow faster and allow more adults to be directly involved in impacting the lives of youth.

Short-term Bible Study Groups

Short-term Bible study groups provide another option for Youth Sunday School. Short-term groups are started for an identified purpose and time frame, with a specified end date and an intentional focus on reaching the unsaved, building relationships, and promoting spiritual growth. Witnessing is an intentional part of these Bible study groups, with the goals of leading lost youth to Christ and assimilating participants into ongoing Youth Sunday School classes. Short-term Bible study groups offer several advantages:

Foundational Evangelism 1

- Short-term groups often meet in homes where a more informal atmosphere can be created.
- These groups often appeal to unreached youth who will not attend Sunday School at church.
- Study content can be selected to appeal to youth's needs.
- Most of the participants have something particular in common.
- The groups are not limited by public building space.
- Leader enlistment and member participation may be facilitated by a shorter-term commitment.

Short-term Bible study groups offer unchurched youth an opportunity to move into the church and Youth Sunday School classes. These groups normally dissolve at the end of the study, and youth are invited and encouraged to join an ongoing class. Department outreach-evangelism leaders should develop intentional plans for assimilating these prospects into the ongoing class. The relationships that have been established should make the transition into ongoing classes natural and simple.

Bible study is a spiritual growth experience, a step toward achieving spiritual maturity in Christ. The issue is not when or where Bible study takes place; the goal is to proclaim the message of salvation by meeting to study God's Word. Most people still prefer to meet in organized classes on Sunday morning at the church, but effective Bible study can take place anytime, anywhere.

Short-term Bible study groups provide another option for Youth Sunday School.

Biblical Leadership 5

Remember that Sunday School is not, however, an organization, but a strategy for doing the work of the Great Commission. An effective Sunday School strategy is one in which a ministry environment exists that encourages unsaved people to come to faith in Christ; encourages believers to be intentional, active soul-winners; facilitates life-changing Bible study; builds fellowship among people; and engages people in pursuing the church's functions—all in an atmosphere of grace, acceptance, love, and support.

Chapter 4

Looking at the Leaders:

Build the Leadership and Train Effective Leaders

JARRETT GAZA

The Youth Sunday School leadership team is made up of every youth leader who has been enlisted to work with teenagers in your church. Everyone is a member of the team working to implement the Sunday School strategy. Each person deserves to know the expectations and responsibilities of his or her role. A clear statement of roles and responsibilities can be encouraging to the persons who are considering accepting a position of leadership. When leaders understand what they are supposed to do and can see that they are not alone, but are working as part of a team, they are more likely to respond positively to the call to lead/serve. They also are more likely to be effective and satisfied in their role.

Don was a former professional baseball player. He had also grown up in another denomination and was not familiar with all the "Baptist" stuff we sometimes take for granted. Some viewed Don as an unlikely candidate to be a Youth Sunday School worker—in fact, Don viewed himself that way. When I first contacted him about working with youth in Sunday School, he was reluctant and he gave the standard excuses: *I can't speak in public; I don't know the Bible very well;* and *I'm not sure I want to make that kind of commitment.*

I struck a compromise with Don and asked him to commit to attend a seminar for potential youth workers that included a broad overview of Youth Sunday School along with observation of youth in an actual Bible study session. Don eventually committed to work in Youth Sunday School as a teacher, and within a year, he became a great youth department director.

Don was successful for two main reasons: First, he was recruited properly; then he was given training before he actually had to assume a responsibility in Youth Sunday School.

→ Having a quality Youth Sunday School takes work.

Where Do You Start?

Before enlisting individuals to fill positions in Youth Sunday School, it is important to understand the philosophy of quality Youth Sunday School work. For our purposes here, let's use the acrostic W-O-R-K; because having a quality Youth Sunday School takes work.

W stands for we. Youth Sunday School is a "we" deal, not an "I" deal. We are all in this work together. Youth ministers, youth division directors, youth department directors, or youth teachers who try to build their ministry in Youth Sunday School around themselves are doomed to failure. It must be all of us working together—a team made up of youth, youth leaders, parents, church staff, and other concerned folks in the church. In a later chapter, we will discuss the specifics of the team members' responsibilities.

Family Responsibility

Here's an adage that may help you: "There is no limit to the amount of good a group or individual can do if they don't care who gets the credit." If we all work together to accomplish the purposes described in chapter 1, then we will succeed in our ministry.

O stands for two things: **organism and organization.** When it comes to the workings of the church, there seem to be two extremes. There is one group that views the church as an organism. It is alive, well, moving, changing, dynamic, shifting, and growing. The members speak of the church as the body of Christ and they even have a "spiritual" language that they use when speaking. On the other hand, there are those whose view of the church and Youth Sunday School is that it is an organization. They look at the organization chart and they see that every spot must be filled. Never mind who fills the positions—these folks are committed to the concept of organization. They are the other extreme. It's not that organization is unimportant; it's just that for that group the organization is the most important thing.

Biblical Leadership

Youth Sunday School is an organized organism.

Of course, philosophically, we should land somewhere in the middle of those two extremes. Youth Sunday School is an organized organism. We are alive, well, moving, changing, dynamic, shifting, and growing, but we are also organized. If we want Youth Sunday School to work in our local church we need to see this concept and embody it.

R stands for three things: **respect, responsibility, and resources.** As a leader in the Youth Sunday School's organized organism, I am always on the lookout for other youth leaders. I look for gifts, talents, abilities, passion, and compassion as I seek folks to work with youth. When I go to a person after having recognized those things, and I ask them to consider working with youth, I am respecting the qualities that God has given them. Another word for that is affirming—I affirm their qualities when I ask them to consider taking a job in Youth Sunday School. That is respect.

When they say *yes* and agree to work in Youth Sunday School, I, as a leader, can now hold them responsible to use the gifts, talents, abilities, passion, and compassion to reach, teach, and minister to the youth in their care. The word for that is *accountability.* Once these persons have agreed to work, they must be responsible to carry out their commitment. (As their leader, I may need to ask them what I can do to help them do their work more effectively, but if we are going to get quality Youth Sunday School work done, they are ultimately responsible.)

Biblical Leadership

In another chapter on teaching youth you will read about lots of resources. There are many. Sometimes the choices are so numerous that it is staggering. As we move into the 21st century, more and more Youth Sunday School leaders are going to need to become "resource brokers." Making intelligent choices based on content, needs of youth, the sequence of study, and budget will become increasingly more important. As you read that chapter, remember that you are a "resource broker"; and in order to get the work done, you will have to know what resources are available and how to use them.

K is for **kick.** In order to get quality Youth Sunday School work done, there must be a kick—or a catalyst. As youth leaders, we must function as the catalysts. We must be the ones who jump-start our team into action, and who encourage our youth to be and do what God intends and to light a fire under those who would rather sit on the sidelines. However, to make sure that work is done, we cannot just depend on ourselves to motivate others—we must also depend on the ultimate catalyst, the Holy Spirit. He is the catalyst to motivate us in the directions that we need to go.

Sometimes seniors have more spare time, and they may be more patient and loving with teens than other adults.

Where Are the Leaders?

If you have served on a church's nominating committee, you have probably asked yourself this question on many occasions. As you think about locating people to work with your youth in Sunday School, remember that really good Youth Sunday School takes an investment of time, and there are no easy ways to find and train the workers. Following are some ways to locate potential workers with youth in Sunday School.

- **Keep your eyes and ears open** for adults who relate well to youth in other arenas of church life, and keep a list of those people in your computer. Add to it as often as you can. If you don't have a computer, you can still keep a potential youth worker file. (The point is that you should always be looking!)
- **Don't limit your search** for leaders to younger adults. While it is true that younger adults can relate to youth because they are not far removed from them in terms of experience, seniors have more spare time, and they may be more patient and loving with teens than other adults. Look for potential workers in unusual places like the senior adult department.
- **Ask your current leaders** for the names of persons who might be good youth leaders. Their friends might be the perfect ones for a particular department or class.
- **Check with your youth.** See if there are people in the church whom they admire and would like to have working with them. If we really believe that youth are members of the body of Christ, this is a great way of acknowledging that fact.

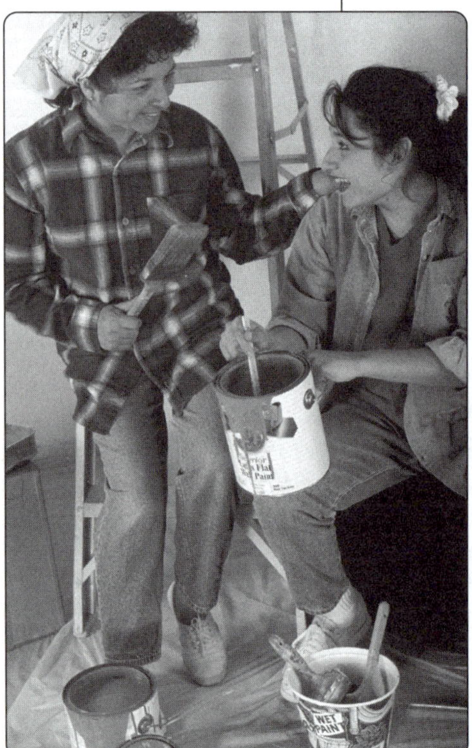

- **Parents are another source** for discovering folks to work with youth. Most parents of teens want to know what is going on in the Youth Division of your church and they might be willing leaders.

3 Family Responsibility

- **Look over your sponsor lists for youth activities.** Many who are willing to go on youth trips as chaperones and sponsors would also be willing to work with youth on a regular basis.
- **Youth Vacation Bible School workers** often are another resource for Youth Sunday School workers. Sometimes when working on a short-term basis they get "bitten by the bug," and decide they would like to work with teens every week in Youth Sunday School.
- **Study the rolls of Adult Sunday School classes** to see who is active and faithful. There may be a person there who is waiting to be asked to work with your teens.
- **Consider having a churchwide survey** in conjunction with other age groups to discover potential leaders. Include on the survey a space where members might suggest names of people who have an interest in youth.
- **Think creatively of other ways** to find those people in your church who are potential workers in Youth Sunday School.

What Adult Workers Are Needed?

In the appendix, you can find complete job descriptions of the various workers with youth in Sunday School. An effective Youth Sunday School organization includes the following positions. (As you read, keep in mind that this is an ideal organization. In your church there may not be a need for every one of these positions; or you may need a combination of these. Fit these positions into your church's organizational structure in the way that best meets the needs of your youth and youth ministry.)

- Minister of Youth.—Ideally, the youth minister should be the lead person in the Youth Sunday School organization.
- Youth Division Director.—Coordinates the work of two or more Youth Sunday School Departments in your church.
- Youth Department Director. —The department director is the coordinator of two or more classes in a department.
- Teacher.—Helps youth discover the truth of Scripture in small group experiences.
- Outreach-evangelism Leader.—Coordinates the work of outreach in a department and provides opportunities for training in outreach and evangelism.
- Secretary.—The secretary keeps records of attendance and other important data on youth. In many churches, the secretary and outreach-evangelism leader are combined into one position.

These jobs in the Youth Sunday School organization are to be filled by adults. Youth serve as class members and class leaders. (See chapter 3.)

5 Biblical Leadership

Wanted: Commitment

Each member of the Youth Sunday School team needs a depth of commitment that will impact the lives of teenagers. Securing that kind of commitment is difficult—the worker needs to know what is expected of him or her, and also what he or she can expect from the leaders. Communicate to the worker what you are willing to promise in the way of support—physically and spiritually—and what you will expect in return. These expectations might include:

- attendance at training opportunities;
- attendance at weekly leadership meetings;
- knowledge of the church's plan for providing supplies, materials, and other support;
- regular attendance at worship services;
- communicating with youth beyond Sunday morning;
- witnessing, ministry, and visitation;
- the need to arrive early and to be present consistently on Sunday morning.

One way of securing this kind of commitment is through the use of a workers' covenant. In dealing with volunteers you need to be careful how you communicate the use of this covenant, but it is a way of getting in writing a commitment from youth leaders concerning their work in Youth Sunday School. Remember that if workers help create the covenant, they will be more likely to stick to their commitments for working in Youth Sunday School.

What Is the Correct Enlistment Process?

Following is a five-step process for getting the right leaders in the right places in your Sunday School organization.

Jesus gives us instructions about how to get the workers: PRAY!

Biblical Leadership 5

Enlist with Prayer

There are two kinds of enlistment: proper and improper. Improper enlistment comes in all kinds of packages. Here are a few examples of improper enlistment:

Pulpit enlistment.—Most of us have had the experience of finding ourselves in desperate need of workers and asking the pastor or minister of education to beg from the pulpit for volunteers to work with youth in Sunday School.

Bulletin or newsletter enlistment.—Much the same as pulpit enlistment, a written appeal through the newsletter may create the same problem of people responding for inadequate or wrong reasons.

Hallway enlistment.—We've all done some hallway enlistment. This is a temporary solution; most likely that person will not last long, and will soon be replaced. The bottom line is this: it's permissible to use these methods to make people aware of our need for youth workers, but these are not satisfactory methods for enlisting workers.

Proper enlistment includes several steps:

- Pray that God will lead you to those who would be good workers with youth. A principle by which I live in youth ministry is that if God gives us the youth, He will also give us the people to work with them. Matthew 9:37-38 states, *Then he said to his disciples, 'The harvest is plentiful but the workers are few. Ask the Lord of the harvest, therefore, to send out workers into his harvest field.'*

Thus, Jesus gives us instructions about how to get the workers: PRAY!

- Prepare a list of the workers you need. Make this an ideal list, aiming to have every position filled. (Don't be discouraged if you don't get every position filled. It's better to have the persons who feel God's leadership filling those positions than to simply have the positions filled with warm bodies).

- Secure approval for your workers through the proper channels in your church—don't circumvent the system. Some churches use the nominating committee as a clearing house: all names of potential workers come through the nominating committee to make sure they are not being asked to work in more than one division in the church. This committee may also be the one that screens nominees to eliminate any potential problems.

Other churches use the nominating committee to actually enlist people for the positions in each division. If this is the procedure in your church, be sure to provide the names of the workers you want to be enlisted for each of the positions. Don't assume that the committee will automatically know whom to enlist.

In some churches, the staff is responsible for filling positions. Whatever system your church has in place to secure workers, be sure to work through that system.

- Schedule an appointment with each prospective worker. It's important to ensure that you have a dedicated time for the two of you to discuss that person's opportunity to work with youth. This meeting may take place in a restaurant, at the potential worker's office, in your office, or in the evening at his or her home. This is the time when you will discuss job descriptions and expectations. Try not to conduct a casual, passing-in-the-hall kind of conversation; what you are asking this person to do is important.

- Take along needed resources for the enlistment visit—a job description, worker expectations (including what the worker can expect of you), class or department roll, copies of curriculum materials, a list of training opportunities, and other helpful materials such as videos. If a prospective worker is to make an intelligent decision, it's only fair to give him or her as much information as possible about what is going on in the Youth Sunday School Division. A discussion of the job description is very important at this point so that, later on down the line, he or she doesn't get blindsided by some expectation you failed to mention to them in the beginning. It's also helpful (and often reassuring!) to tell them about upcoming training opportunities.

• Finally, ask the person you are seeking to enlist to pray about accepting the position. Don't ask for an immediate decision—allow time for them to ponder the decision. Say that you will get back in touch with them soon, and give a specific time frame (a week or ten days, perhaps). Be sure to call them back at the appointed time.

For many of us, the greatest difficulties come in trying to enlist people to work in junior high or middle school. Once when I was an eighth-grade department director, I had an especially hard time recruiting an eighth-grade boys' teacher. (Those kind of people are not easy to find!) Someone told me I should ask Ray. Ray has a Ph.D. from Rice University, and what does a person who has a Ph.D. from Rice have in common with eighth-grade boys? But remember I was desperate, so I contacted Ray and went through the previously outlined process. I came down to the last step and asked Ray to pray about the decision; he assured me that he would. I contacted him several days later, and asked him for his answer. His response was, "I've prayed about that, and I'll do it." (Ray worked with eighth-grade boys for two years.) The process works. God will provide the workers if we will seek to enlist them properly.

> If a prospective worker is to make an intelligent decision, it's only fair to give him or her as much information as possible.

Equip Them

There are around 100,000 Youth Sunday School workers in the Southern Baptist Convention. From years of leading conferences and consulting with youth workers, I've discovered that many of the questions about curriculum, methodology, or the purpose of Youth Sunday School can be traced back to two things: the worker hasn't received any training to do what he or she was enlisted to do; and there is no regular planning time for all of the workers to meet together.

Our job in Youth Sunday School as youth ministers, division directors, Sunday School directors, and ministers of education is to provide training for those we have enlisted. Proper enlistment is great, but without training we set ourselves (and them) up for failure.

Emphasizing training communicates to our workers the importance of effective Bible study; it says that we are committed to do what it takes to reach and teach youth as Jesus would have us do. At best, it is difficult to keep a youth ministry up and running. When workers are properly enlisted and trained, however, everything (and everyone) functions more efficiently.

Biblical Leadership 5 As leaders, we want to leave a legacy of quality youth work so that when the teenagers of today become adults they will have a strong desire to teach teenagers themselves.

Any person who wants to work in Youth Sunday School should have some initial training. Don, the teacher mentioned earlier, is a prime example of a successful teacher who was trained and enlisted properly. Instead of being handed a leader guide and a list of youth in his class, (the way many teachers are recruited) Don was trained in what to expect in a Youth Sunday School class and department. He understood what the purpose of Youth Sunday School was. (See chapter 1 for this information.) He got some idea of what kind of youth he would have in his class by studying age group characteristics; he received a job description, and knew what was expected of him as well as of the other members of his team; he even received a preview of the materials that he would be using on Sunday morning. Encouragement was given him to be in attendance at the weekly leadership meeting and provision was made for him to have some opportunities for fellowship with other members of the Youth Sunday School team. All of these things were included in Don's initial training.

There is another kind of training that is equally important—ongoing training. With ongoing training, provision is made for workers to be updated on new materials and methods, to be given opportunity to understand the planning process better, and to be encouraged to grow spiritually as they try to be the best workers possible.

Where do our workers get training? Several sources come to mind, but here are a few:

- *Self-guided study.*—Youth Sunday School workers should take advantage of the excellent resources that are available for training. Right now you are reading a book that can be a self-guided study. Every year LifeWay Christian Resources publishes materials that are designed to train workers in some aspect of their work with teens—including understanding youth, teaching philosophy and methods, ministry, and evangelism. See the *Youth Ministry Catalog* or our website, *www.youthscape.com*, for the current resources available.

> **Without training, we set ourselves (and our workers) up for failure.**

Biblical Leadership 5

- *Local Church Training.*—Many churches provide annual or semiannual training events to equip their workers to be better teachers. Often these experiences are based on the same materials that an individual could read or work through on his or her own, but the group study provides interaction and involvement.
- *Associational Training.*—Many associations provide regular times of training for age group Sunday School workers (usually in fall and spring). The events may take place at different churches each year, but the training is available. Most associations have an associational consultant team with an age group specialist who is equipped to train youth workers. That consultant will come to your church to train your workers. Contact your associational office for more details about this great training opportunity.
- *State Training.*—Many state conventions provide regional or statewide training opportunities for all age groups. Check your state convention's training schedule for dates when you and your workers can receive this quality training.
- *National Training.*—LifeWay Christian Resources of the Southern Baptist Convention provides several excellent training opportunities that are national events. Conference Centers like Glorieta, New Mexico, and Ridgecrest, North Carolina, provide annual, multiple opportunities for youth workers to receive outstanding training for their responsibilities in Youth Sunday School.

Training for Youth Sunday School workers is readily available to those who desire it. If you want to have a team of the best possible youth workers, commit to training—both initial and ongoing—in order to work effectively with teenagers in the 21st century.

Enable Them

A person may be enlisted properly and given the proper training to be an effective youth leader, but without the right resources it will be extremely difficult to be effective.

Most youth workers I know would be unable to take a passage of Scripture and with complete understanding of the needs of teenagers, the meaning of the passage, a knowledge of various learning-teaching approaches, how God uses His Word to teach, and a proper sequencing of the study, be able to do an effective weekly Bible Study for a specific group of teens. So, using curriculum material that is already prepared (with all of those things and more), makes more sense than trying to develop a study of their own each week.

Spiritual Transformation 4

Since there is a lot of curriculum material available, we leaders need to become "resource brokers"—using the limited financial resources that we have to provide the best possible materials for our Youth Sunday School workers to lead their classes and departments. Make it your priority to train people in the use of the materials that you provide for them.

Empower Them

One of the most difficult and risky things for a leader to do is to empower his or her followers to do the work. Turning a teacher or department director loose requires faith on the part of the leader. But remember the preceding outline—if you have enlisted a person properly, provided the necessary training for that person to do his or her work, and you have given them the resources for teaching teens, you can be assured that they are ready to launch out on their own. Let them do it with your blessings!

- Have a Youth Sunday School worker recognition service.
- Publicly affirm your workers in all kinds of settings.
- Tell them personally of your appreciation of their work with teens in your church.

A word of encouragement goes a long way in keeping the workers that you have, and it also builds long-term loyalty to the youth education ministry in your church.

Expect Great Things From Them

When you do these five things you can expect people to do great things in youth ministry—and they will do it. They will not be perfect; none of us is. But most people will do a good job. I'm convinced of that, and my experience has proven it to be true.

What About the Role of the Youth Minister in All of This?

It is my contention that the youth minister is not only to be the educator of the youth and the youth leaders in the church, he or she is also to be the educator of the *parents of youth* as well. It is not that the total responsibility for parent education rests in the lap of the youth minister, but he or she does have an obligation to make sure parents know what is going on in the lives of their teens and to give the parents help in rearing teens. The youth minister does not have to be an expert in parenting nor does he have to have children who are teens. He can act as a concerned person in providing information and training for parents in the rearing of their teens.

3 Family Responsibility

→The youth minister should be the chief advocate for Youth Sunday School.

The youth minister is also the educator of the church and staff regarding Youth Sunday School. He or she must be the person who helps them become aware of what takes place in the Youth Sunday School ministry. The youth minister should be the chief advocate for Youth Sunday School.

What to Do with an Ineffective Worker

All of us in youth ministry have had to deal with workers who are ineffective or who do not function as team players. Although this is not a pleasant subject, it is one that needs to be addressed—so here goes!

Those people who work with teenagers deserve the same attitude of grace and mercy that we would afford a teenager who may be less than what God would desire. Occasionally, workers have circumstances in their lives that cause them to be less than effective and they have no control over the circumstances. Some examples are difficulties at work, conflicts at home, or overcommitment in the community or church. There are other times when the leader just has not had proper training or the encouragement to get training, and they are ineffective as teachers and leaders. Following are some guidelines for what Bob Taylor (Youth Consultant from Nashville, Tennessee) calls "disenlisting" workers.

1. Share your philosophy of youth education often. If it is shared early and often, some of your people will disenlist themselves.
2. Transfer them to another place in youth ministry where their gifts will be more effectively used.
3. Make a special effort to build a relationship with the person.
4. Treat a person whom you are disenlisting like you would want to be treated.
5. Organize your Youth Sunday School in such a way that volunteers enlist and manage volunteers.
6. Make sure that your pastor (or other staff to whom you are responsible) knows of your desire to disenlist the person. They may know of circumstances that affect the way a person is teaching.
7. Never go by yourself to a disenlistment appointment. Always have someone go with you to lend prayer support.
8. Ask the person for suggestions as to what you can do to help him or her better serve in another area.
9. Keep on praying for the right words to say and the right attitude to exhibit.

Are you a baby-sitter or an equipper? What is your philosophy of youth ministry? Some people feel that youth ministry should primarily be a provider of activities for their youth to keep them busy. We who work in youth ministry have higher goals.

Being a baby-sitter or just keeping youth busy will not equip them to be what God desires them to be as members of His kingdom. As a Youth Sunday School leader, it is part of your job description to educate and encourage each youth on his or her road to spiritual maturity. To serve as an equipper of youth is one of the highest callings of God!

Your Own Spiritual Growth

The leader is the lesson applies to your relationship with other youth leaders as well as your relationship to the teenagers you teach! When your spiritual life is in good relationship to God, it is easier to discern His will as you seek to enlist quality leaders to join the Youth Sunday School team.

5 Biblical Leadership

At lunch one day, I discussed youth ministry with a prominent youth minister and his wife. He leaned across the table and, in all sincerity, expressed to me that often he would wake up in the morning knowing how much had to be done, and would forego his quiet time with God in order to get to the tasks of his youth ministry.

I don't believe this person is an exception in youth ministry. In fact, this may be the norm for many who have the responsibility of nurturing our youth. It certainly isn't a deliberate decision not to spend time with God; it just seems to sneak up on us. This omission is subtle, and it can be devastating!

The principle of biblical leadership states that Sunday School recognizes that *the leader is the lesson* in that every leader is accountable for being an authentic example of Christianity in personal living and producing new leaders for service through the ministries of the church.

If, as a long-time youth minister, I had to choose only one thing to share with you as a youth leader, this would be it: Don't neglect your own spiritual pilgrimage.

Don't neglect your own spiritual pilgrimage.

Your Quiet Time with God

It doesn't matter what you call it (*quiet time, time alone with God, daily devotionals, daily Bible reading, spiritual growth time*), the discipline of spending time on a regular basis with our Lord keeps us growing as Christians.

R. Clyde Hall, Senior Manager of the Discipleship and Family Youth Section at Lifeway Christian Resources shares four reasons for spending time with God.

1. **To Maintain Fellowship with God.** When you and I became Christians, we entered into an eternal relationship with the Lord that no one can take away from us. However, in order to enjoy the benefits of that relationship (fellowship) we need to spend time with the One with whom we have the relationship. The best illustration of this is my own relationship with my wife. Connie and I have been married 27 years. Imagine if, after our marriage in Brownwood, Texas, she had gone to San Francisco and I had gone to New York. Imagine that for 27 years we didn't speak to each other, we didn't write to each other; we didn't communicate with each other in any way. Even though we were legally married, what kind of relationship do you think we would have? Obviously, not much of one! It's a good thing to spend time with the ones you love, and it's a better thing to spend time with your Savior.

One other illustration to impress this point in your mind: I am a sports car enthusiast; the only way to enjoy driving a sports car is to maintain the car so it will run properly. Unfortunately, my cars have spent more time in our garage than out on the highway because they were not always properly maintained. This is what can happen to your relationship with God if it is not maintained. You lose the benefit of the power, the exhilaration, and the experience when you neglect spending time with Him.

2. **To Build Spiritual Strength.** Have you faced a difficult temptation in the last few days? One with which you really grappled? If you have, you probably used an enormous amount of spiritual energy to overcome that temptation. One reason to spend time with God on a regular basis is to rebuild the strength that gets drained every time we deal with a temptation. I would encourage you to decide that time spent with the Lord will build your strength to be an effective agent for Him.

4 Spiritual Transformation

3. **To Become Spiritually Sensitive.** A little over seven years ago I came to work for the Baptist Sunday School Board (now called LifeWay Christian Resources of the Southern Baptist Convention). For 10 years prior to my decision to come, I was contacted every time there was an opening for a consultant in the Youth Sunday School area. For 10 years I did not sense that God was opening up that door for me. Then about eight years ago some circumstances happened in my life that opened up a door, and as I read my Bible and spent time with God, He began to make it very clear to me that He wanted me to take that job. At no time in that whole process did God send me a telegram. Nor was it written in His Word that I should move to Nashville, Tennessee. However, because I had been spending time with Him, the direction was clear. Spend time with the Lord to develop a spiritual sensitivity to His leadership in your life.

4. **You can't lead others in a direction you are not going yourself.** Not one of us would say to a youth, "You don't need to grow as a Christian." None would indicate that a young person ought not spend time with God on a regular basis. We

5 Biblical Leadership

> God desires a relationship with us, and it cannot be governed by the clock.

know from our experience and from God's Word that it is essential for us to spend time with Him. Many youth leaders are guilty of trying to guide youth and youth parents in a direction that we ourselves are not traveling. Ultimately, they will have to make their own decision about the priorities in life, but we youth workers can lead by example as we are committed to our quiet times.

When Should I Spend Time with Him? Many individuals feel that early morning is the only proper time for a quiet time. I disagree—we're talking about a relationship. I would never say to one of my daughters, "I can only spend time with you at a specific time." It's true that occasionally we have a planned night out together, but I want them to feel free to spend time with me whenever they can.

Some folks are morning people. (I'm one of those!) Early morning is my regular time to spend with Him. However, there are many times when I want and need to spend a few moments with God before I go to bed at night, and I often do that, too. Can you think of a better way to end a busy day than to lay your head on the pillow after reading God's Word and talking with Him? I can't.

We live in a mobile society. Many of us spend a lot of time in our cars or on a plane. I often find myself talking with God as I travel. Obviously, I can't read the Bible while I am driving, but I can speak with Him as I drive down the road; many people also use this time to listen to Christian music or devotionals on tape.

Just remember: God desires a relationship with us, and it cannot be governed by the clock. Spend time with Him when it is best for both of you. It is helpful to have one regular time each day—discipline is good for our lives!

Where Do I Spend Time with Him? Several years ago I read a devotional entitled, "Any Old Bush Will Do." The thrust of that devotional was that God can speak to us anywhere we are willing to listen. For Moses, it was at a burning bush. For you it may be at your desk, your dinner table, or in a comfortable chair. I have known many youth who not only did their homework on the floor of their rooms but they also spent time with God there, too. The location is not important, as long as it is comfortable. The kitchen table is my place; it has been helpful through the years to have a certain place where I meet Him daily.

What Materials Do I Use to Spend Time with Him? There is a wealth of excellent devotional material available, and many people have favorite authors or favorite compilations for devotional reading. Through the years there have been times when I used several different resources in order to keep my time with the Lord fresh; perhaps you do the same. Just remember to make sure the Bible is the primary resource for your time alone with its Author. Some excellent resources available through Lifeway are *Open Windows* and *essential connection.*

Is There a Recommended Process for Spending Time with Him? If you have a schedule that works, keep using your own. It is helpful for youth who make a commitment to a quiet time to give them a suggested outline. The following has been helpful to me.

1. **Pray.** Spend some time asking God to reveal His thoughts to you as you read His Word. I often find myself asking God to let something "leap off the page" at me—and this has happened many times.
2. **Read.** Read God's Word. There are many devotional plans available, but the

best resource is God's own Word. Most devotional books structure the daily thoughts so each page begins with a passage of Scripture on which the devotional thought is based. Read His Word first.

3. **Write down** what God says to you in His Word. Writing is a helpful discipline because it helps articulate what we discovered from our reading and prayers. Journaling is a great way to enhance your relationship with Him. Any notebook will serve this purpose, but I have found the *DiscipleHelps* journal to be useful.

4. **Pray again.** This time write down your prayer. Let it reflect what you have discovered out of His communication to you. The sentences don't have to be complete and you needn't worry about others reading your prayer. What you write is between you and God.

5. **Write an application statement.** This may be the most difficult thing that you do in your time with God. In your journal, be as specific as possible about what you will do with what you have discovered in your prayer and reading of the Scripture. (*A change of attitude, or an action you will take, for example.*) Sometimes it helps accountability to share your decision with a trusted friend or another youth leader.

6. **Read the devotional thought.** See if what you discovered from God's Word is the same as what the devotional writer discovered. Most of the time, you and the writer will come up with different messages. I often feel that God wants me to get something different from His Word. That is encouraging to me.

7. **Pray.** Close out your time with Him by praying about the whole process. Did He tell you that you needed to change a relationship, confess a sin, or correct a wrong? Ask for His strength to accomplish what He desires. Find what it takes to spend some quality time with the Creator of the Universe and then do it!

> Write down what God says to you in His Word.

Your Personal Stewardship

As you keep yourself in growing condition as a Christian, try to be a good steward. What is involved in stewardship? A tithe should be the initial commitment that we make regarding our finances. Other commitments we make with our money ought to reflect God's leadership as well. Seeking God's guidance about how we spend our money is the wise way to be a good steward of the material wealth that God provides us.

There are other aspects of life that mustn't be neglected:

• *Your physical body.*—A good steward takes care of what God allows him to have, and that includes your body. Getting proper rest, exercise, and eating the right food are some simple ways to maintain your body for God's sake.

As a youth minister, I have kiddingly said that lock-ins are "of the devil"—my energy level after a lock-in is almost nonexistent. Lock-ins take an enormous amount of energy, and frequently there is very little to show for them after they have happened. Even though I personally don't care for them, I do know some youth ministers who have used lock-ins effectively to reach youth in their communities. The point is this: Be careful how you use the energy that God gives you. We need to plan to use our energy for His glory and benefit.

• *Your time.*— We only have 24 hours a day, 7 days a week, around 30 days a month, and 365 days a year. How we use our time is important to God. Being a good steward of our time may mean that we cut out some of the meaningless activities in which we participate, and devote more time to His work.

• *Your influence.*—Do you realize there are many people who look to you as an example of how the Christian life should be lived? Besides the countless youth who look up to you, you may not be aware of parents of teens or other church members who see you as an example of Christ's life to them. Being a good steward of your influence has huge ramifications for the kingdom of God.

Your Faithfulness to Worship

When I lived in Texas, I served a church that for a period of time met in a junior high school for Sunday School. The school was about five blocks from our main campus, and we had over 200 youth and youth leaders who were meeting there each Sunday. Before Sunday School we had to make sure everything in the school was set up and ready for us, and then after Sunday School, we had to make sure that the school was left in good shape for the classes that would meet there on the next day. It was important to me to keep a good relationship with the school, so I spent a lot of time making sure everything went smoothly. Guess what soon happened? Because I was focused on cleaning up the school after Sunday School, I started missing the worship service back at church. One Sunday I realized that I was drying up because I did not have a time when I was worshiping with the rest of the church body.

Being a good steward of your influence has huge ramifications for the kingdom of God.

Youth Bible Study takes a lot of administration. The subtle temptation is to focus on the nuts and bolts of Sunday School and our own personal preferences concerning church participation—resulting in our neglect of the really important aspects of our Christian life. Don't fall into that trap! We cannot be true to the biblical principles of spiritual transformation and biblical leadership if we neglect our own personal worship—private and corporate.

Your Personal Witness

Foundational Evangelism

In my own spiritual pilgrimage, I tend to think that if I am teaching, preaching, or speaking, I am doing enough to fulfill the command to be a witness. And, in fact, I am witnessing. But the problem is that sometimes I use those activities as an excuse for not witnessing in other ways and at other times in my life—as Jesus would have me do. For example, my home ought to be a place where I am a witness; my community ought to be a place where I am a witness; my arenas of influence ought to be places where I am a witness. Here is an experience to illustrate that point:

I have three beautiful daughters, and our house seems to be a boy magnet! One young man in particular started coming to my house as the boyfriend of one of my daughter's best friends. We struck up a relationship, and before long Sam had broken up with his girlfriend, but continued to come to our house—a lot! Sam attended our church with his former girlfriend, but he was not a member of our Sunday School. I became convinced that I needed to witness to this young man. God's spirit really dealt with me, and as a result of many circumstances that were, I believe, orchestrated by God, when Sam was in our home one night, I asked him about his relationship with Christ. Before the evening was over, Sam had invited Christ into his life to be his Savior. The point of sharing this story is not to point to myself or to my daughter (who regularly invited him to church); it is to remind you and me that we have a responsibility to witness at places other than in the church house or at youth events. God desires that I be His witness wherever I go.

Don't neglect your own spiritual pilgrimage. For some reflection time look up and read 1 Corinthians 9:24-27.

Chapter 5

Implement the Strategy: Provide Space and Equipment, Value Record Keeping, and Develop Soul Winners

Chapter 3 of this book dealt with planning the strategy of Youth Sunday School. The intent of this chapter is to look at the implementation of the strategy. How do we get the work done?

The principles of foundational discipleship and biblical leadership urge us, as Youth Sunday School leaders, to plug into the mission of our church and to encourage our youth and youth leaders to be "fully involved in the church's overall mission."

Your church and Sunday School may choose to launch the new church year by having a Launch Weekend. A Sunday School Launch Weekend includes several events designed to prepare individual Sunday School leaders and mobilize all members for the challenges and opportunities of the new year. During this weekend, Sunday School leaders celebrate accomplishments, communicate plans, train and commission leaders, and create a sense of excitement and purpose about the upcoming year. This can be an exciting time as youth leaders join their church in evaluation, planning, and setting goals. All Youth Sunday School leaders should be encouraged to attend the activities and to participate in special training for Youth Sunday School work. See chapter 5 of *Sunday School for A New Century* for more detailed information on a proposed schedule for this event.

Weekly Sunday School Leadership Team Meetings

Weekly Bible study necessitates weekly planning. If we want to make a difference in the spiritual lives of youth, we should never settle for "traffic light" planning. (See chapter 3.) A Bible study planning meeting can include these areas of preparation:

- sharing information about youth activities and ways workers can be included
- setting department goals
- evaluating what worked and what didn't in the previous session
- evaluating the next session's procedures and deciding what to use
- working on outreach ministry or a fellowship
- working on budgets, special projects, visuals, prospect rolls, or inactive youth
- coordinating space needs, resources, and schedules (See Appendix for recommendations on space and equipment for Youth Sunday School classes and departments.)
- praying together.

5 Biblical Leadership

→ Weekly Bible study necessitates weekly planning.

What takes place in a weekly Sunday School leadership team meeting? Who is in charge? How can I get my workers to come to one more meeting?

These are FAQ's (Frequently Asked Questions) at training conferences. In all honesty, many Youth Sunday School teaching teams do not have weekly planning meetings because they don't know the answers to those questions! In the next few paragraphs you will find some suggestions about what to include in your planning meeting; and each week in the leader guide there are additional suggestions for specific session planning. Use the plan sheet (found in the appendix) as a guide for conducting the meeting; it is also helpful to have a printed agenda for each meeting. For additional information on monthly and weekly planning, see section 5 of *Sunday School for A New Century.*

The Focus of the Meeting

Prayer should permeate the discussion in each area of work.

Each segment of the weekly leadership meeting is to contribute to the achievement of the objectives of Youth Sunday School. Instead of a separate prayer period in which prayer tends to become generic, prayer should permeate the discussion in each area of work. This allows for more specific and focused praying about issues and people.

- *Focus on the Mission* (10 min.).—This portion of the meeting provides an opportunity to relate the work of the Sunday School departments and classes to the mission and the ministry of the church. Information is shared concerning the church's ministry. Leaders are made aware of churchwide emphases, needs, and concerns and how they can support or address them.
- *Focus on Relationships* (25 min.).—During this time, relationships with members and prospects are discussed, individual needs assessed, and—as appropriate—plans are made to involve members in responding to them. Approaches are determined for being involved with members and prospects beyond the Sunday morning session, especially ways to involve members in evangelism. Specific plans are made for fellowship activities and various assimilation actions to involve members and prospects in loving and caring relationships. Visitation reports and assignments may be shared.

Biblical Leadership 5

Churches using the FAITH Sunday School Evangelism Strategy will use this time to review assignments, give reports, and make follow-up assignments. Occasionally during this time, a study and review of witnessing approaches may be conducted.

- *Focus on Bible Study* (25 min.).—Teaching for spiritual transformation is facilitated when leaders work together to plan the best way to bring members into a life-changing encounter with the Bible message. Bible study is the focal point around which people are reached for Christ and becomes the foundation for leading people to evangelism, discipleship, fellowship, ministry, and worship. During this time, previous Bible study sessions may be evaluated, assignments made for subsequent studies, and in particular plans deciding how the Bible content for subsequent Sundays will be taught. Make sure that all workers know what each person is doing, so that the department director does not "steal the thunder" of the teacher or vice versa. Think together and creatively about how to involve youth in the process of Bible study.

But When?

When can we squeeze in another meeting?

That's another frequently asked question! The best meeting time is that which fits the needs of the church and the people who are to participate. The meeting time chosen needs to be coordinated with other church leaders. Generally, a minimum of one hour needs to be set aside for the meeting. The best case scenario happens when your church reserves a time on Wednesday night to allow age groups to plan without other meetings interfering. If Wednesday night is not possible for workers in your department, consider other options—Sunday afternoon before the evening service, during dinner before visitation, Sunday lunch after the morning worship service, or a weekday evening in a worker's home.

Once weekly leadership meetings are begun, make every effort to maintain that time as a valuable, productive hour. Stick to the agenda, communicate clearly, provide resources, continue to evaluate and set goals. If youth leaders perceive the meeting time to be valuable, they will be faithful in attendance and commitment.

Outreach-Evangelism

The first step toward reaching people is to understand, accept, and practice Matthew 22:37-39. *Love the Lord your God with all your heart and with all your soul, and with all your mind . . . Love your neighbor as yourself.* Simply stated, if we love God, we want to do His will. If we love our neighbors, we will want to see them saved and at work in God's kingdom. This is the primary motivation for outreach.

Foundational Evangelism 1 Pray for unchurched teenagers; lead your class/department to pray specifically for:

- a desire to see lost youth saved (especially those whose names are in the prospect file);
- opportunities to get to know lost teenagers;
- ways to encourage or meet specific needs;
- ways to share Christ with specific lost teenagers.

→When you pray for someone, it is important to know how to pray specifically.

Unchurched teenagers are not looking for the friendliest youth group in town—they are looking for friends. When you pray for someone, it is important to know how to pray specifically. In getting to know that person, you need God's direction. Pray for direction on how to get to know that person better; pray for ways to discover this person's needs because meeting needs will draw people together; pray to God for direction in meeting the needs you discover. You may even let the person know you are praying for him or her. Sometimes the person you're praying for may tell you some of the things he or she wants you to pray about. While praying in the above ways you can always keep in mind the goal of sharing your faith. (A perfect opportunity to use the FAITH Sunday School Evangelism Strategy training!)

Prospect Discovery

Identify youth whom you can reach through the Sunday School. Where and how can you find those youth?

Many strategies give ways to obtain prospects for Youth Sunday School. You cannot reach someone unless you have a name and other vital information. Here are some ideas:

•Conduct a prospect survey by canvassing a certain area to obtain names of the unchurched. The church office or church outreach-evangelism leader can filter names to the Youth Sunday School of unchurched teenagers who visit church worship services. Concerned adults can share names of youth they know who are not involved in a church.

Foundational Evangelism 1

• The best way to discover names of unchurched youth is through Youth Sunday School members themselves. They know youth in their schools, on their teams, in their clubs, and other places teens find themselves.

• Attend school activities. Study school annuals or club rolls. The schools are the most significant mission field you have when it comes to unchurched teenagers. Make an effort to meet the friends of the teenagers in your Youth Sunday School.

• Check church pictorial directories and membership rolls. Many times adult church members have teenagers who do not attend church. Many unreached youth may already have a connection to your church.

• Take advantage of fellowship parties and activities. Encourage youth in your Sunday School to bring unchurched friends. Youth Sunday School workers may also consider planning activities designed especially for members to bring unchurched friends.

• Develop a church web page. Web sites can serve as places where prospects can find your Youth Sunday School. Many families have personal computers and use the Internet often. Churches are finding that web pages are good tools in providing information about their Youth Sunday Schools.

• Identify unchurched children from Vacation Bible School. When those unchurched children promote to seventh grade, they become prospects for seventh-grade Sunday School. Seventh-grade Sunday School workers and the youth minister might also consider working with sixth graders in Vacation Bible School to establish relationships with those pre-teens.

Foundational Evangelism 1

• Plan special Bible study events and short-term groups to reach unchurched youth. See Chapter 6 for help in the section called, "What About Other Bible Teaching Events?"

Keep Up with Them!

As prospects are located, good record keeping will be vital. Make sure to secure pertinent information on all youth who visit your Sunday School and other program organizations and activities. When possible, record information on their families as well. Youth Sunday Schools should have some type of registration card to obtain the necessary information. A variety of registration cards is available through LifeWay Christian Stores.

Once you have information on prospects and unchurched youth, be sure to place that information in a prospect file. The prospect file has been described as the lifeblood of Youth Sunday School. This file is used by the outreach-evangelism leader to make prospect assignments to other Youth Sunday School leaders. Many churches have family prospect files where information on the entire family unit is kept. The information from this file is filtered to different age division files. In many cases, this information is computerized. The computer generates prospect information that can be passed on to Youth Sunday School leaders or members. If your church already has a system in place, make good use of it. If not, plan on starting a prospect file for Youth Sunday School, or at the very least, your class or department.

3 Family Responsibility

Another popular prospect file system is the pocket and card system (available through LifeWay Christian Stores). Even if your church has no system in place, you can develop your own system using something as simple as note cards, a card file, or shoe box. Make sure you record as much vital information on youth prospects as possible.

At a minimum you would want to know the name, address, phone number, date of birth, grade, school, family information, and the date you received all of the information on the prospect. For youth prospects, it is helpful to know their interests, activities, sports/club involvement, email address, and so on. If the prospect visited your Sunday School or another event as a guest of one of your members, you might find it helpful to record whose guest they were. Once a prospect file has been established, the outreach-evangelism leader and department secretary should work together to make sure information is accurate, useful, and available. Prospect files should be kept current and up-to-date.

Cultivate Prospects

Once prospects are discovered, reachers must take time to cultivate them. Cultivating these young people and their families will take time and effort on the part of a reacher. There are a number of things that can be done to cultivate prospects; however, you should first begin with prayer.

- Inviting prospects to class functions will give them an opportunity to experience fellowship with class members and build relationships.
- As a youth worker, you yearn to show all teenagers how and why Jesus is the answer to all their needs, and you wonder where you will find the time and energy to reach each one for Christ. Start with a few; each time you see or hear about specific teens, ask God for opportunities to reach them. Choose ten to be your "most wanted youth." Record facts about these youth, actions you take to reach them, and results of the outreach actions. Include their school name and names of parents/guardians. You may want to put this information on index cards or have a notebook with a sheet for each youth.
- Mobilize your youth. Youth can reach youth in ways adults can't, and adults can reach youth in some ways that other youth can't.
- Enlist youth individually to go with you to visit. Avoid asking groups of youth to go on witnessing/prospect visitation. As you apprentice youth by taking them along with you one at a time, they will gain confidence and witness more freely on their own. They will also be glad you chose them to go with you.
- Share information on other family members with adult, children, and preschool leaders. Be sure to coordinate visits with other age groups.
- To cultivate parents of youth, take information about your church and consider giving parents a copy of the magazine "Living with Teenagers."

→Mobilize your youth to reach other youth.

5 Biblical Leadership

Basic Types of Visits

- *Prospect Visitation.*—Visits to youth who are not enrolled in Bible study
- *Evangelistic Visitation.*—Visits to youth in order to share the promise of Christ
- *Absentee Visitation.*—Visits to inactive youth and chronic absentees
- *Ministry Visitation.*—Visits to youth to meet specific needs
- *Family Member Visitation.*—Visits to family of members and youth prospects
- *Member Visitation.*—Visits to youth who are active in Bible study. Too often, these youth are taken for granted. They need to know they are appreciated.
- *Spontaneous Visitation.*—Visits that are not planned. Although you do need to plan to be intentional in your outreach, occasionally you will have opportunities to make spontaneous visits. These are visits you make to prospects or members when you just happen to be in their neighborhood or at a place where they are. These visits can, at times, be very productive. Take advantage of these spontaneous times.
- *Student FAITH visitation.*—For churches that participate in the FAITH Sunday School Evangelism Strategy, there are evangelistic and ministry visits.

Foundational Evangelism 1

How many teenagers do you come in contact with and have meaningful conversations with every single day? If you are like most youth workers around the country, you probably do not come in contact with very many teens on a regular basis. But now, ask yourself this question: *How many teenagers do the teenagers I teach on Sunday morning come in contact with and have meaningful conversations with every single day?* The answer is staggering! Your students come in contact with hundreds of teens every day! So another part of the good news is that the youth in whose lives you invest are actually investing themselves in the lives of many other teens.

Your students come in contact with hundreds of teens every day!

Some Ideas for Effective Outreach

Create a Tutoring Service.—If you have interested youth and adults, sponsor a free study hall or tutoring service on selected days during the week or month. Serve refreshments, and let your studious youth help. (They can serve or tutor.) Get to know the unchurched youth who come.

Foundational Evangelism 1

Campus Christian Clubs.—Many campuses have Christian clubs that can be instrumental in ministering to and reaching teenagers for Christ. With the encouragement of some significant, key youth workers or club sponsors, these clubs can be student-led. Consider the following steps:

1. Enlist six students to start the club. Students should consist of a leader, an assistant leader, and four other students.
2. Challenge the six students to enlist six other like-minded students from various areas of influence. For example, a student from the band or student council could be instrumental in influencing others from the band or student council to participate in the club.
3. Provide the club with Bible study materials, such as "Campus Connection" in *essential connection*, or help students develop their own.
4. Encourage clubs to meet for a limited number of weeks (10 weeks is suggested) in the fall and the spring. A limited number of weeks helps the club keep momentum through the year.
5. Limit the length of the Bible study to approximately 45 minutes. Follow the study with a time of fellowship or fun.

6. Adult sponsors meet with the club student leaders occasionally for prayer, encouragement, support, and problem solving. Adults can occasionally attend meetings to support the student leaders and meet unchurched youth.

Unchurched youth who attend Christian club meetings can be filtered into your Youth Sunday School.

→ Unchurched youth who attend Christian club meetings can be filtered into your Youth Sunday School.

Pop-in Visitation.—Pop one bag of microwave popcorn for each visit you intend to make. After allowing steam to escape from the popped bag, fold over top of the bag and punch two holes. Cut curling ribbon (one yard for each bag of popcorn) and place the end of the ribbon in each hole that has been punched. Tie a bow and curl the dangling ends of the ribbon. Enlist a teenager to deliver popcorn to prospects or absentees. This is also a good thing to be delivered during an exam week.

Car Wash.—Use your church's parking lot to hold a free car wash for any youth's car in your city. Require the youth to complete a card (name, address, church affiliation) to get the free car wash. Once they hand in the card, wash their car (the better the job, the better the impression). Once the car wash is over, sort through the cards and develop a prospect list.

Prayer Breakfast.—Ask youth to meet for prayer and devotional thoughts one morning a week at a fast-food restaurant. This may be combined with a regular jogging program before the meal. Encourage youth to bring lost or unchurched friends.

The Unprogram.—Enlist youth to be involved in a mentoring relationship with youth workers and other adults. This apprentice-type relationship will allow them to observe adults sharing their faith "as they go." Youth should always be enlisted to help with the preparation of youth events, such as buying groceries for camps and retreats; adults should model witnessing experiences for youth as they interact with those involved.

For many more great ideas for outreach and visitation, see *Good News for Youth, The Power to Change Lives*, by David Scott (available at LifeWay Christian Stores) or visit *www.youthscape.com.*

Accomplishing the Work

How does this all work? As we consider our purpose in Youth Sunday School let's use the analogy that as workers we are "player/coaches."

Evangelize.—As a youth worker, my job is to evangelize youth and those who influence them. That means that I am in the game trying to evangelize as many as I can (I'm also a player), but since I don't come in contact with many teens in a single day, my job also includes equipping youth to evangelize their friends. I am to help them learn how to share their faith with others. That makes me a coach.

To enable you to be a better coach, here are two suggestions:

- Encourage youth *to* witness to their friends. (You can provide a plan of salvation, using one of many simple plans—there is one in the front of the learner's guide for Sunday morning Bible study.)
- Encourage youth *when* they witness to their friends. Provide all kinds of support and incentives when they have taken the time to share with their friends. We cannot neglect this second part because it so vital to the equipping process.

Foundational Evangelism 1

Disciple.—Another word for the verb *disciple* might be *mentor*. I am to guide youth in discipleship and eventually to become disciplers themselves. Again, using the player/coach analogy, I'm in the game myself when discipling them. But I'm also coaching them to become disciplers. This may be a long, hard process, but it is biblical and it is imperative (2 Tim. 2:2). My prayer is that they will see in me what I want them to become as Christians.

Family Responsibility 3

Fellowship.—One of my goals is to guide youth to fellowship with each other, and that includes equipping them to know what fellowship is and how to do it. Teenagers love the warm feelings they have at camp or at the late-night sharing time at a lockin or DiscipleNow weekend; but frequently they mistake those feelings for genuine fellowship. Unfortunately, those events sometimes center around "getting things off their chest," or "confessing the wicked, evil, mean, and nasty things" they did before becoming a Christian. Two suggestions are appropriate for youth leaders: Remind youth to keep their focus on the Lord and what He is doing in their lives instead of on themselves and how bad they were; and give them some guidelines for sharing at times when emotions are running high. Examples of those guidelines:

- Ask youth to tell one thing that God is doing in their lives;
- Ask youth to tell one thing they see God doing in their Sunday School youth group;
- Ask youth to share one thing they see God doing in the life of one of their friends;
- Ask youth to tell one thing for which they are grateful.

These four activities will serve to keep the focus on God and away from them. It also can provide calm in the midst of emotional storms.

The investment we make in a few of our students can pay great dividends to the masses of teenagers with whom they interact daily.

Minister.—I am to minister to youth and their families, but I am also to equip them to minister to their friends. (Teenagers certainly shouldn't act as professional counselors, but often they can be of great help to their peers by being a trusted listener.) This equipping task can be an involved process such as establishing a peer ministry; but it may also be as simple as helping youth know how to make a ministry phone call, how to write a ministry note or affirmation card, or how to make a ministry visit to a home or hospital. Remember—teenagers have contact with many more youth than we do, so the investment we make in a few of our students can pay great dividends to the masses of teenagers with whom they interact daily.

Foundational Discipleship 2

Worship.—As a youth leader, my desire is to guide youth to worship; but I also want to equip them to know how to worship. Once again, I must be an active participant in both personal worship and corporate worship. In addition, I will equip teens to know how to do both, providing them with materials and instruction so that they may have the most meaningful worship experience possible.

Chapter 6

Teaching for Spiritual Transformation:

Teach to Transform, Conduct Special Events, and Choose Sound Curriculum

By Richard Barnes

Whatever you have learned or received or heard from me, or seen in me—put it into practice. And the God of peace will be with you (Phil. 4:9).

"Mark, what are you doing with that shovel in Sunday School?"

"I'm using it to teach the seventh-grade boys."

"They've gotten that bad, huh?"

"No, it's not that. Romans 6 is a hard passage for seventh graders to understand. We are going to take the Scripture to a real practical level today—we're going outside and bury the sins that Christ has put to death in us. We'll list the sins on slips of paper, dig a hole and bury the papers. I think the guys will get the point."

What a great teaching idea! Those seventh-grade boys will tangibly see, touch, and discuss the meaning of Romans 6. And because they were actively involved in the lesson and related the biblical truth to something they were already familiar with (burying objects) they will very likely remember the truth of Romans 6—at least until the following Sunday!

Remembering a truth is one thing; obeying the truth is another. The boys will soon encounter a real-life test of their belief in the truth that Christ has put to death their sinful attitudes and habits. The test may come that Sunday afternoon with their family or on Monday morning at school with their peers. Assuming they remember the Bible truth, will they obey the Lord by saying *yes* when they have the opportunity to honor their parents or to witness to a lost friend or to reach out to befriend a new student?

→Remembering a truth is one thing; obeying the truth is another.

How can we teach youth God's Word in such a way that they will be motivated to examine the Scriptures and apply it obediently to their lives in all their relationships? To answer this question, we need to know:

- who we are in Christ as leaders and teachers;
- why we teach youth the Bible;
- who the youth are;
- what to teach them;
- how God uses His Word, us, and other resources to teach them.

Who Am I to Teach These Students?

As a leader, are you confident of who you are in Christ?

In chapter 1 you read about what should motivate adults to teach youth—love for God (Mark 11:29-30) and obedience to the Great Commission (Matt. 28:18-20). How do I deal with those times when I don't feel love for God and even struggle with whether I want to continue teaching?

The first way to be ready for such difficult times is to believe God's Word about who you are in Christ as a believer and leader. There are many references in the New Testament to the position that believers have by virtue of their faith in Christ. Let's focus only on a few truths from John 15. First, John 15:1-5 states that, as a believer, you are part of the true vine and you are a branch through which Christ can bear fruit. Jesus said that you must remain in close fellowship with Him to continue to bear fruit, and you must allow the Father to bring discipline to your life to bear more fruit. But look at what you become as you remain in Christ—not just His servant, but His friend (John 15:15)! Now reflect on what Jesus said about you and the great promise about prayer in John 15:16: *You did not choose me, but I chose you and appointed you to go and bear fruit—fruit that will last. Then the Father will give you whatever you ask in my name.*

Biblical Leadership 5

Earlier in this book we examined the importance of leadership. Twenty-first century Sunday School leaders recognize that the leader is the lesson—every leader is accountable for being an authentic example of Christianity in personal living and producing new leaders for service through the ministries of the church. *A student is not above his teacher*, Jesus said, *but everyone who is fully trained will be like his teacher* (Luke 6:40). The question is not whether you will teach, but whether you will be a good teacher—one worth imitating. Reflect again on Philippians 4:9 at the beginning of this chapter.

Why Teach Youth the Bible?

Foundational Discipleship 2

As you learned in Chapter 1, Sunday School is the foundational strategy in a local church for leading people to faith in the Lord Jesus Christ and for building Great Commission Christians through Bible study groups that engage people in evangelism, discipleship, fellowship, ministry, and worship. Every Christian's life objective is to make disciples. Disciples are like apprentices, who possess both intellectual understanding and personal skills to fulfill a certain task. As apprentices, disciples can themselves become disciple-makers of others. The place where you can introduce youth to foundational discipleship is found in the Bible study group called Sunday School.

In Matthew 28:18-20 there are actually three words and phrases that modify the command to "make disciples." The first is *go* (v. 19). *Go* can mean get out of the routine of your daily life and set aside specific time and energy to go to where youth are. It can also mean *as you go* through the responsibilities of your everyday life.

The second phrase is *baptizing them in the name of the Father, the Son and the Holy Spirit.* Baptism symbolizes conversion and new birth. Great Commission teachers intentionally seek to lead people to salvation through faith in Christ and lead these new believers to proclaim that faith publicly in baptism.

Let's spend a little more time on the third phrase, *teaching them to obey everything I have commanded you.* Note that teaching is an essential part of the Great Commission. In the Great Commission both the goal and the content of teaching are identified. We are to teach youth "to obey" and we are to teach them "to obey everything" Jesus commanded. There's no part of the Bible that youth should not be able to study.

Sunday School champions the absolute truth and authority of the Word of God and compels believers to integrate a biblical worldview into their minds, hearts, and lives through ongoing systematic Bible study. The goal of Bible study is transformed lives that exhibit love for God and others (Matt. 22:37-40; 1 Tim. 1:5). Such lives glorify God and are Christlike in nature (Ps. 119:1-16,105-112; 2 Cor. 3:18; Col. 3:16-17).

Can you see God raising up this generation to impact our world unlike any previous generation?

Who Are These People?

Chapter 2 in this book examined the wonderful (and yet sometimes tragic) world of today's youth. Sunday School recognizes that Bible study is most effective when it

Spiritual Transformation 4

occurs in the context of the learner's total life, especially family relationships, and when it considers the age and developmental life needs, generational perspective, current life issues, special needs, and learning preferences of the learner.

Unfortunately, the reality in our youth ministries and Youth Sunday Schools at the end of the 20th century is that few seem to be living what they are taught. Search Institute reported that 88 percent of youth workers declared that helping youth apply faith to daily decisions was "very important" but only 25 percent said they did it "very well."[1] In 1997 the Discipleship and Family Division of LifeWay conducted a survey of more than 2,500 youth who attended summer youth conferences. The results indicated that of these predominantly active Southern Baptist youth:

- almost one-fourth have thought about killing themselves,
- three-fourths have trouble with their tempers, and
- half cheat on tests.

At the same time, though:

- 78 percent don't drink,
- 83 percent don't take drugs, and
- 93 percent pray "daily" or "weekly."

Clyde Hall, leader of Youth Discipleship Training, said, "It's shocking to know that some of the kids who think about killing themselves are the same kids who pray either daily or weekly."[2]

Is something not connecting here? How could teenagers who have been in such strong Bible study and discipleship groups and who go to week-long summer camps pray daily or weekly and then cheat on tests or think about killing themselves? Have we been caught in the trap of settling for short-term knowledge of biblical content and "getting through the lesson" while neglecting the longer-term goal of Jesus' Great Commission to teach them obedience—"to obey everything I have commanded you" (Matt. 28:20)? Have we been so focused on how youth learn that we have neglected how God

Family Responsibility 3

teaches them? Can we adult leaders team up with parents and other family members of youth to become co-workers with God to change the way youth think, feel, and act? Yes, God can use you (and me) to teach youth God's Word in such a way that their lives and ours are spiritually transformed.

What Do I Teach Them?

The Bible is the textbook for Youth Sunday School. The Bible's purpose is not just to inform but to transform (John 20:31). Teaching youth the Bible means leading them to interact with God's Word in a ministry environment that is conducive to the Holy Spirit's work of spiritual transformation. *Spiritual transformation is*

God's work of changing a believer into the likeness of Jesus by creating a new identity in Christ and by empowering a lifelong relationship of love, trust, and obedience to glorify God. Twenty-first century Sunday School teachers recognize that teaching does not stop when the session ends; it is a seven-day-a-week strategy for involving learners in seeking the Kingdom of God and fulfilling the Great Commission.

4 Spiritual Transformation

Teaching youth the Bible for spiritual transformation starts before the session, is heightened during the session, and continues after the session.

Twenty-first century Youth Sunday School teachers use the Bible, depend on the Holy Spirit, seek to teach God's Word in and through the youth's family, magnify relationships with youth, accept accountability for living what they teach, and seek to lead youth to be accountable for their own spiritual transformation. (For help on choosing curriculum, see the appendix.)

How Do I Teach Them?

As we move into the 21st century, we must engage learners in a biblical model of instruction that leads to spiritual transformation. In the New Testament, *instruction* includes commands or directives, and the word has an "edge" to it, adding a sense of urgency and passion. In contemporary life, instructors typically deal with issues that change people's lives and warn of the consequences of failing to follow certain principles and guidelines. A flight instructor is a good example: Flight instructors teach pilots with intensity because not only is the life of the pilot at stake, but the life of the pilot's passengers are on the line. Bible instructors or teachers intentionally lead participants to the spiritual "fork in the road" that calls for participants to personalize the truth, struggle with it, believe it, and obey it.

Easily stated, but challenging to execute, here are three "best practices" for 21st century teaching:

- Before the teaching session, *prepare* the ministry environment for spiritual transformation.
- During the session, guide the learners toward spiritual transformation through an *encounter* with God's Word in a youth Bible study group.
- After the session, *continue* to guide learners toward spiritual transformation in daily living and family relationships.

4 Spiritual Transformation

First, prepare! (2 Tim. 2:15)

As you learned in chapter 3, all effective Sunday School leaders are prepared. The apostle Paul directed in 2 Timothy 2:15, *Do your best to present yourself to God as one approved, a workman who does not need to be ashamed and who correctly handles the word of truth.* There are two ways to get prepared: through Sunday School leadership meetings and through personal Bible study and prayer.

Beyond the Sunday School leadership meeting, you must also prepare personally for God to use you to teach His Word. As you prepare for the Bible teaching session, ask God to speak to you personally about your own walk with Him.

As you and your fellow Youth Sunday School leaders plan together, seek to prepare a ministry environment conducive to spiritual transformation. A ministry environment includes the teaching-learning environment, but it is much more. Yes, you will want to give attention to the physical setting—walls, chairs, and visuals, for example. But you will want to create an atmosphere in which youth feel welcome and wanted from the moment they arrive. Focusing on relationships and individual needs, including family concerns, is key to preparing the environment for caring for youth through love and teaching God's Word.

3 Family Responsibility

As you prepare the teaching plan, you will want to develop the session in such a way that youth are motivated to examine the Scriptures and apply them obediently to their lives in all their relationships. Such preparation includes a solid understanding of not only how youth learn but, more importantly, how God uses His Word to effect spiritual transformation.

Seven Bible Teaching Elements

There are seven Bible teaching elements that can guide us in a Bible study process that leads to spiritual transformation. These seven elements should guide your personal Bible study as you prepare for the Bible teaching session. The seven Bible teaching elements will rarely be completed before the end of a 60-minute Bible study session, but for the Holy Spirit to transform lives, all elements will be experienced by participants before, during, and after the session. The amount of time devoted to the seven Bible teaching elements will vary based on the different youths' life situations. While some youth may need these elements in specific, sequenced steps, other youth may prefer that the elements occur in a different sequence or repeatedly throughout the session. The elements can be repeated throughout a session or over a period of several lessons in a unit, much like a spiral advances upward through a series of repeated movements.

There are seven Bible teaching elements that can guide us in a Bible study process that leads to spiritual transformation.

- Acknowledge Authority (*control*).—What authority, power, or rule guides the life of each youth?
- Search the Truth (*content*).—What did God say in the Scripture to the first readers or hearers?
- Discover the Truth (*concept*).—What abiding truth(s) for all generations is the Holy Spirit teaching from the Scriptures?
- Personalize the Truth (*context*).—Based on the abiding biblical truth(s), what is God teaching me about thinking, feeling, and living today?
- Struggle with the Truth (*conflict*).—What conflict or crisis of belief is the Holy Spirit bringing about in my heart and life to challenge what I think and value and how I live?
- Believe the Truth (*conviction*).—How is the Holy Spirit leading me to live and repent—to change my mind, my values, or the way I live—or to resolve the conflict?
- Obey the Truth (*conduct*).—To what extent will I obey the Holy Spirit's leadership in what I think and value and the way I live?

(For a study from John 4:1-42 on how these seven Bible teaching elements found expression in Jesus' teaching ministry, see *Sunday School for a New Century*, available at LifeWay Christian Stores.)

Second, Encounter!

During the session, guide the youth toward spiritual transformation through an encounter with God's Word in a Bible study group. For 21st century biblical instruction, we will take the following tried and true principles to a new level. Specifically, let's inject the following new meanings into these terms.

- Total Period Teaching.—The concept that teaching and learning can occur before the session, during the session, and after the session. In short, teaching youth the Bible is a seven-day-a-week strategy.

• Central Bible Truth.—The "Biblical Truth" that is the focus of the study before, during, and after the session.

• Youth Needs.—Starting with where youth are right now in their developmental, social, and generational concerns, seek to discern what God's message is for youth through this study. A "Life Question" could help youth grasp the significance and relevance of the Bible passage and biblical truth. Ultimately, the Bible study should address the authority that rules what youth think, believe, and feel and the way they behave. What will the youth conclude is God's message for them through this study? What inner conflicts and struggles will be created in their lives as a result of exposure to the biblical truth?

A "Life Question" could help youth grasp the significance and relevance of the Bible passage and biblical truth.

• Knowledge Teaching Aim.—The biblical content (what the Bible said to its first readers) and biblical concepts (understanding what the Bible means in terms of eternal principles) usually examined during the Bible study.

• Application Teaching Aim.—The "Life Impact" that identifies ways learners could give evidence of spiritual transformation in their lives—their love, trust, and obedience that glorifies God. Such application moves beyond making a mental connection of a biblical truth's relevance to obedience seven days a week as leaders and learners struggle with the truth, believe the truth, and obey the truth.

• Motivate Youth to Study the Bible.—The teaching plan steps that grab the attention of youth based on where youth are "coming from" in order to engage them more readily in the Bible study session. Every participant comes to a Bible teaching session with an authority—recognized or unrecognized—that controls his or her life. Leaders and teachers also recognize that they are engaged in a spiritual warfare for every youth's mind, heart, and life. This beginning step in the ministry environment attempts to focus every youth's attitude and intention to learn a biblical truth that connects with their lives.

• Examine the Bible Passage.—The teaching plan steps that engage youth in the Bible Passage by searching the Scriptures for biblical content and biblical concepts that can be personalized for life today.

• Apply the Bible to Life.—The teaching plan steps that continue to help youth personalize the truth. Inevitably, youth will experience inner conflict as biblical truth intersects with contemporary life. Application is not complete until this conflict is resolved by change of belief, attitude, and action as reflected in a lifestyle of love, trust, and obedience that glorifies God.

Note: While "Examine the Bible Passage" and "Apply the Bible to Life" steps are usually separated, they are interrelated. Never wait to guide youth to personalize the truth and struggle with it just because you are not under a heading that says, "Apply the Bible to Life." Be sensitive to the Holy Spirit. He can begin leading youth to a point of conviction at any point during the Bible study session!

Teaching-Learning Approaches

The role of the teacher is to guide learning in ways that facilitate the work of the Holy Spirit to transform lives. This includes recognizing the ways in which learners learn best (1 Cor. 3:1-2; Heb. 5:11-14). Teaching youth God's Word will more likely bear fruit when you relate to them with teaching-learning approaches they prefer. Teachers must seek to connect not only with the learner's mind but also with the youth's heart. Wise teachers employ a variety of approaches to reach the hearts of youth.

Biblical Leadership 5

A major part of motivating youth to study the Bible begins with preparing the physical setting for the Bible study. Consider this real-life example from Youth Sunday School:

Joey: "What's going on here? Why is everyone looking at the ceiling?"

Teresa: "Look at the poster Gilbert did for this Bible verse! He put it on the ceiling!"

How many students do you think looked at that poster? How motivated do you believe the youth were to know what Gilbert believed about that verse?

Here's yet another real-life example of making the room a tool for teaching: During their Sunday School leadership meeting, Ruth and her eighth-grade Sunday School teachers got excited about the upcoming Bible study on overcoming spiritual obstacles. On Wednesday night before Sunday, they turned the tables and chairs over and scattered them around the room. When students arrived on Sunday morning, they would have to go over or around tables and chairs to get to the food. Ruth and her colleagues were looking forward to a "teachable moment."

When Ruth arrived at church on Sunday morning 15 minutes early (like every good youth leader should!), she was shocked! Yes, the maintenance staff at the church—being the conscientious employees they were—rearranged the room in the usual fashion! Because Ruth and others were there early, they still had time to set up their room for a stimulating Bible study on overcoming spiritual obstacles.

Examine the following list. To discover a time when Jesus employed each of these teaching-learning approaches, read carefully Luke 22:1-38, Luke 9:57-59, and Matthew 26:30. You will find each of these teaching-learning approaches at least once in those passages of Scripture.

- Relational.—These learners are highly social, make friends easily, and may be very good talkers.
- Musical.—They enjoy listening to music and often find it easy to express themselves through music—composing, playing, and performing.
- Logical.—They see patterns and can reason through difficult situations.
- Natural.—These youth enjoy being out-of-doors and can readily identify elements of the natural world.
- Physical.—These students are usually active and prefer to get involved through methods such as drama, field trips, and sports.
- Reflective.—They understand who they are and how they feel and may prefer to work alone.
- Visual.—They can "see" in their minds as well as in the concrete world. They also enjoy creating their own pictures and visual representations.
- Verbal.—These youth like to use words—either reading, writing, speaking, or listening. They often enjoy poems, stories, debates, monologues, and essays.

Now think about the youth you are assigned to teach. By which of the above ways does each prefer to learn? The truth is that your group of youth may have every one of these different learning approaches present during any given Bible study session. Also, no individual learns through only one of these approaches. As the leader, don't limit how the Holy Spirit can break through to a teenager by choosing only one or two approaches to teaching.

You can learn to relate creatively to this generation's language, culture, and life issues. Ask the youth to help you; the key is variety. Avoid getting in a rut. (In case you haven't heard, a rut is a grave with both ends kicked out.) The death knell for a youth Bible study group is the label, "boring." Avoid doing anything—even the "most fun things"—the same way every Bible study session.

Relational learners are highly social, make friends easily, and may be very good talkers.

Probably the strongest factor expressed as necessary for keeping youth involved in Sunday School was variety.

Some teaching-learning approaches are more effective in department time, when all classes meet together in a large group. Other approaches may be more effective in class time, when you have only a small group of youth together. If your Youth Sunday School is large enough for both departments and classes, vary the opening activity between department time and class time. Better yet, stay in department time or class time the entire period, especially if the nature of the study lends itself more to a large-group approach or a small-group approach.

In February 1998, this is what 35 youth and 25 adults in Mississippi said about teaching youth: "Probably the strongest factor expressed as necessary for keeping youth involved in Sunday School was variety. The youth desired variety in format, activities, and teaching styles. They expressed feelings of boredom and a lack of interest toward doing things 'the same old way' week after week. The unexpected, unusual and unpredictable created the feelings of missing something if they missed Sunday School."[3]

See the appendix for a listing of Youth Bible Teaching-Learning Approaches that can help you choose the best approach for motivating youth to examine the Scriptures and apply them through obedience in all life's relationships.

The word *believe* carries with it more than intellectual assent. In the Bible, believers showed their faith by acting on that faith. In recent years, almost everyone has insisted on Bible study resources that "apply the Bible to life."

Third, Continue!

Spiritual Transformation 4

Because teaching doesn't stop when the session concludes, continue your teaching ministry "24-7", 24 hours a day, seven days a week. After the session, continue to guide youth toward spiritual transformation in daily living and family relationships. Because Bible teaching that leads to spiritual transformation extends beyond the teaching session itself, *continue* means helping the students connect the everyday experiences with the larger picture of what God has planned for their lives.

Continue means getting the Word of God off the page and bringing it to life in the minds and hearts of the students. Learning occurs all the time, and some of the best learning experiences are spontaneous. Try to continue teaching by helping youth connect with what they already know. When students can see that God's "abundant life" plan for them is spiritual transformation into Christlikeness, they will have a framework that the Holy Spirit can use to help them make sense of their day-to-day problems, questions, victories, and joys. As their teacher, you should continue your teaching ministry in whatever context you can—at school activities, in conversation with parents and other family members, on church trips, in one-on-one times. You may choose to enlist youth as class leaders within the Bible study group to help you with this third essential.

Based on their Bible study and in obedience to the Holy Spirit, you could use questions such as these to explore with them after the session in conversations, cards, letters, or emails:

What command did God present?

What promise did God make?

What truth did God teach?

What attitudes, behaviors, or values will you make a part of your life?

What relationships are you developing in your life that are a part of your journey of becoming a Christlike believer?

Family Responsibility 3

As you "continue" to teach, you will have opportunity to work with the families of youth. Much of what influences youth in Sunday School is beyond your control—the amount of support students receive in their families and the kind of acceptance and affirmation they get from peers and at their schools. Nevertheless, you must do all you can to connect with home, friends, and school. Sunday School affirms the home as the center of biblical guidance and helps equip Christian parents to fulfill their responsibility as the primary Bible teachers and disciplers of their children. Get to know the parents of your youth. Pray with them and for them. Tell parents what you are studying and ask them what they observe their teenagers putting into practice from God's Word. Also, encourage parents to be involved in their Sunday School classes.

3 Family Responsibility

Why Should I Use a Learner's Guide?

To help youth get the most out of Bible teaching-learning before, during, and after the session, take advantage of the most strategic tool other than the Bible itself—the learner's Bible study guide, sometimes called a "quarterly" or a student book. Bible study guides for youth are designed to:

- provide youth with features on how to become a Christian and live for Christ. What other resource, week in and week out, better communicates the primary purpose of an "open" Bible study group than a well-designed learner's guide that prominently features the plan of salvation?

1 Foundational Evangelism

- help youth develop Bible knowledge and Christian convictions based on sound biblical exposition. Where else can youth learn more consistently what the Bible teaches on the Christian faith? In *21 Truths, Traditions, and Trends*, Bill Taylor addresses the importance of a learner guide as a "constant monitor of doctrine."[4] He stresses that today's Sunday School learners are being bombarded with many varieties of false teachings and adds that many churches have almost abandoned leadership training for teachers, leaving teachers to teach tenets that could be detrimental to sound biblical doctrine. Learner guides provide the "true compass north" on biblical doctrine.
- encourage youth to develop life-long Bible study skills and Christian disciplines through providing Bible study helps. What better way is there to help youth learn to study the Bible, pray, and feed themselves spiritually on their own than through a well-planned learner guide?

→ **Learner guides provide the "true compass north" on biblical doctrine.**

- provide youth attractive visuals that engage them in reflective questions and biblical insights. How often do youth find photography and illustrations that beg them to examine and integrate God's Word?
- challenge youth to make a personal commitment to obey what God is teaching them. What tool will you provide after the session for God to use to reinforce the truths you teach on Sunday morning to help them to love, trust, and obey God in their daily lives?
- support a diversity of learning preferences. How will youth "learn it all" during a single Sunday School session? When will youth who prefer to learn alone have their best opportunity to learn and obey the Scriptures?
- provide leaders with an economical tool for involving youth during the session for Bible research and response. Instead of reading from the leader guide, teachers can distribute the learner guides at "teachable moments" in the session and engage youth in reading a drama script or stating their opinion on a case study or photograph. Such ideas will be found in leader guide teaching plans. How much does it cost in time and church resources to prepare or duplicate one-page handout in comparison to multi-page 4-color resources that are economically priced? How much does it cost in time and church resources to prepare or duplicate a one-page handout in comparison to multi-page full-color resources that are economically priced?

→To strengthen your Bible study experience, provide a Bible study guide for each participant and prospect.

• assist youth in preparing for Bible study sessions. Where is the best place to introduce youth to the next session's Scripture passages?

To strengthen your Bible study experience, provide a Bible study guide for each participant and prospect. Use the learner guide in the Bible study session as a tool for exploring the Bible passage. Show youth how to use the learner guide as a spiritual growth resource after the session.

Finally, hold them accountable for obeying what God teaches from Sunday to Sunday. Every Bible study participant expects the teacher and other leaders to come prepared to teach God's Word. What would happen if every teenager came to Bible study prepared to report on what God taught them or how God used them in ministry during the preceding week? What a way to transform Sunday School!

Want Some "EXTRA!" Help?

Do you want to grab the interest of youth in Sunday School with creative teaching tips that use illustrations from recent worldwide news stories, publications, and contemporary music? Since 1991 LifeWay Christian Resources has provided Youth Sunday School leaders with updated motivation and application options to enhance their weekly Bible teaching. Youth EXTRA! is available through *www.youthscape.com* and *www.lifeway.com* on the Internet. Simply retrieve the appropriate file, print it, and give copies to your Youth Sunday School teachers. EXTRA! files are written weekly and are available on the Wednesday before you conduct your weekly leadership meeting, whether it is on Sunday or Wednesday. For more information visit *www.youthscape.com*.

What About Other Bible Teaching Events?

Foundational Evangelism 1

You recall that one of the strategic principles from Chapter 1 is that Sunday School encourages Bible study in short-term groups and through special Bible teaching events. Such special Bible study groups are effective ways to promote outreach and evangelism and to address specific life concerns, spiritual issues, church functions, and doctrinal issues. Bible study groups can be held anywhere, any time you can gather youth. The following list includes the most common special Bible study groups and events:

• *Youth January Bible Study.*—Formerly known as Winter Bible Study, both non-Christian youth and active youth can be targeted for this annual Bible study project. This study of a Bible book or portion of Bible book addresses biblical content at a more intense level without neglecting relationships of those truths to teenagers' lives. And because the adults are studying the same material, Youth January Bible study supports the principle that the home is the center of biblical instruction. Weekday, weekend retreats, or DiscipleNow events can be times to engage youth in January Bible Study.

• *Youth Vacation Bible School.*—While youth are often key leaders in assisting in conducting VBS with children and preschool, youth can also be reached during the summer through a special Bible study project targeted just to them. You can adapt the creative theme that comes with each year's Youth Vacation Bible School resources. By doing so, you can promote it to be one of the key outreach events of the summer to reach lost youth. In the Youth VBS materials available from LifeWay, you will find all you need for leading the event in one Youth VBS teaching kit, including a video that utilizes the best in contemporary Christian music, reproducible masters, posters, recreation and worship ideas, and even ideas for food. You could plan this

five-session event during a single week, conduct it over a series of weeks, or do the study as part of an end-of-school or back-to-school retreat. Youth VBS materials would also work well in a Mission VBS setting because the focus is on outreach. Finally, Youth VBS supports the principle of family responsibility because all ages study basically the same Scripture content.

1 Foundational Evangelism

• *Campus Clubs, the "campus connection".*—Because of Equal Access laws granted to students attending public schools in the United States, students may begin a campus Bible study group as long as other such non-curricular groups are permitted. Such Bible study groups must be student-initiated and student-led. Students involved in this growing campus club movement will find in the center of *essential connection* magazine four Bible studies every month that they can lead.

• *Youth Bible Study Groups During the Week.*—As an adult leader, you know that many youth will not come to traditional Sunday School on Sunday morning. Indeed, students can be reached for Christ through special short-term Bible study groups that focus on issues or Bible books. To help you reach or teach youth beyond Sunday morning, LifeWay Christian Resources provides a variety of resources that may be used in a weekly Bible study, a retreat, a DiscipleNow weekend, or even a lockin. To see the latest resources, consult your literature order forms, *www.youthscape.com*, *www.lifeway.com*, or the most recent youth ministry resources catalog.

3 Family Responsibility

How Can You Improve?

Periodic evaluation of your Bible teaching ministry is critical for extending your Sunday School ministry. You can learn from both your mistakes and your successes. What's the best way to improve?

1. Use the Sunday School leadership meeting as a time to reflect on how to improve all five functional areas of Youth Sunday School: evangelism, discipleship, fellowship, ministry, and worship. Be sure to study attendance records and note patterns in the youth.

5 Biblical Leadership

2. Analyze how well your Youth Sunday School is doing in addressing the five strategic principles found in the Introduction: foundational evangelism, foundational discipleship, family responsibility, spiritual transformation, and biblical leadership.
3. Periodically—at least annually—review the 10 best practices found throughout Chapters 3-6: Identify the strategy. Organize with purpose. Build the leadership. Train effective leaders. Provide space and equipment. Value record keeping. Develop soul winners. Teach to transform. Conduct special events. Choose sound curriculum.

Listen carefully to what youth, parents, and other church leaders are saying. While you will likely not get many positive affirmations from the youth themselves, just one "Thank you!" or hug or smile will keep you going for a long time. Finally, listen carefully for the evaluation that every Christian leader longs to hear: "Well done, good and faithful servant" (Matt. 25:23)!

---

[1]Based on Search Institute's 1995 study, *The Attitudes and Needs of Religious Youth Workers: Perspectives from the Field.*

[2]"1997 Youth Survey." Youth Discipleship Training Section, LifeWay Christian Resources, 127 Ninth Avenue North, Nashville, TN, 37234, 1997.

[3]"Summary Report from Youth Bible Study Forum" conducted with 35 youth and 25 adults in Mississippi about teaching youth; February 1998, as reported by Mark Lott, Consultant, Youth Work, Leader Training Equipping Team, Mississippi Baptist Convention Board, Jackson, Mississippi.

[4]Taylor, Bill. *21 Truths, Traditions, and Trends.* Nashville: Convention Press, 1996. 158-159.

Appendix

The following pages may be duplicated for use in studying this book.

- A New Definition of Sunday School for the 21st Century
- Strategic Principles for 21st Century Sunday School Ministry
- Youth Sunday School Plan Sheet
- Physical Resources Provide a Positive Environment
- Youth Sunday School Job Descriptions
- Three Essential Best Practices of Bible Teaching for Spiritual Transformation
- Seven Youth Bible Teaching Elements
- Choosing Curriculum
- Approaches to Learning and Teaching for Youth
- Teaching Plan

A NEW DEFINITION OF SUNDAY SCHOOL FOR THE 21ST CENTURY

SUNDAY SCHOOL IS
THE FOUNDATIONAL STRATEGY
IN A LOCAL CHURCH
FOR LEADING PEOPLE TO FAITH
IN THE LORD JESUS CHRIST
AND FOR BUILDING
GREAT COMMISSION CHRISTIANS
THROUGH BIBLE STUDY GROUPS
THAT ENGAGE PEOPLE IN
EVANGELISM, DISCIPLESHIP,
FELLOWSHIP, MINISTRY,
AND WORSHIP.

STRATEGIC PRINCIPLES FOR 21ST CENTURY SUNDAY SCHOOL MINISTRY

Five fresh Sunday School principles and related best practices are reflected in new Sunday School leadership curriculum resources released in 1999. These five principles, along with the new definition, identify the primary messages to communicate regarding Sunday School for a New Century.

Foundational Evangelism 1

THE PRINCIPLE OF FOUNDATIONAL EVANGELISM

Sunday School is the foundational evangelism strategy of the church.

1. Sunday School emphasizes ongoing, open Bible study groups that reproduce new groups as the best long-term approach for building a ministry environment that encourages unsaved people to come to faith in Christ, assimilates new believers into the life of the church, and encourages believers to lead others to Christ.
2. Sunday School provides the most efficient churchwide evangelism training network to equip members to become passionate soul-winners.
3. Sunday School encourages Bible study in short-term groups and through special Bible teaching events as effective ways to promote outreach and evangelism and to address specific life concerns, spiritual issues, church functions, and doctrinal issues.
4. Sunday School creates a great center for missionary power as people tell and live the wondrous story of Christ's redeeming love.

Foundational Discipleship 2

THE PRINCIPLE OF FOUNDATIONAL DISCIPLESHIP

Sunday School is the seven-day-a-week strategy for involving people in seeking the kingdom of God and fulfilling the Great Commission.

1. Sunday School provides the primary organizational framework for involving families and individuals in the comprehensive work of the church including evangelism, discipleship, ministry, fellowship, and worship.
2. Sunday School provides foundational discipleship and encourages members to strengthen their Christian walk by participating in other discipleship opportunities.
3. Sunday School emphasizes that every member who is a believer must become accountable for the responsibility God has given him or her as a minister and missionary to the world.
4. Sunday School supports all other church ministries and intentionally encourages its members to be good stewards, fully involved in the church's overall mission.

Family Responsibility 3

THE PRINCIPLE OF FAMILY RESPONSIBILITY

Sunday School affirms the home as the center of biblical guidance.

1. Sunday School helps equip Christian parents, including single parents, to fulfill their responsibility as the primary Bible teachers and disciplers of their children.
2. The Sunday School encourages Christian parents who by word and deed guide their children to integrate the Scriptures into their lives influencing how they think and act.
3. Sunday School involves families in the comprehensive work of the church.
4. Sunday School works to nurture sound and healthy families and seeks to lead non-Christian parents to Christ.

Spiritual Transformation 4

THE PRINCIPLE OF SPIRITUAL TRANSFORMATION

Sunday School engages learners in the biblical model of instruction that leads to spiritual transformation.

1. Sunday School affirms that spiritual transformation is God's work of changing a believer into the likeness of Jesus by creating a new identity in Christ and by empowering a lifelong relationship of love, trust, and obedience to glorify God.
2. Sunday School champions the absolute truth and authority of the Word of God and compels believers to integrate biblical worldview into their minds, hearts, and lives through ongoing systematic Bible study.
3. Sunday School recognizes that Bible study is most effective when it occurs in the context of the learner's total life, especially family relationships, and when it considers the special needs, generational perspective, age, and life-stage characteristics, and learning styles of the learners.
4. Sunday School addresses transcultural life issues common to individuals, churches, families, tribes, and nations regardless of geographic, ethnic, or language identity.

Biblical Leadership 5

THE PRINCIPLE OF BIBLICAL LEADERSHIP

Sunday School calls leaders to follow the biblical standard of leadership.

1. Sunday School affirms the pastor as the primary leader in its ministry of building Great Commission Christians.
2. Sunday School calls leaders to a prophetic ministry, listening to God's voice, discerning His message, integrating the message into their lives, and proclaiming His truth through His church to the nations.
3. Sunday School recognizes that the leader is the lesson in that every leader is accountable for being an authentic example of Christianity in personal living and producing new leaders for service through the ministries of the church.
4. Sunday School recognizes that planning is essential to implementing its strategy.

YOUTH SUNDAY SCHOOL PLAN SHEET

PREPARE the ministry environment for spiritual transformation

(10 min.) FOCUS *on the Mission*

(25 min.) FOCUS *on Relationships*

(25 min.) FOCUS *on Bible Study*

As a youth leader, how does this Bible study address my life as I:

- **Acknowledge Authority**—*What authority guides my life for this issue?*
- **Search the Truth**—*What did God say in the Bible?*
- **Discover the Truth**—*What abiding truth is the Holy Spirit teaching me?*
- **Personalize the Truth**—*What is the Holy Spirit teaching me about thinking, feeling, and living today?*
- **Struggle with the Truth**—*What conflict is in my heart?*
- **Believe the Truth**—*What do I need to change: mind, values, the way I live?*
- **Obey the Truth**—*How much will I obey the Holy Spirit?*

PRAYER CONCERNS

YOUTH SUNDAY SCHOOL PLAN SHEET

ENCOUNTER God's Word in a Youth Bible study group

Teaching-learning approaches for helping youth:

- Get started into the session
- Get into the Truth
- Get the Truth into us

CONTINUE teaching-learning in daily living and family relationships

RESOURCES NEEDED/ PERSONS RESPONSIBLE

PHYSICAL RESOURCES PROVIDE A POSITIVE ENVIRONMENT

The physical and emotional environment influence learning both directly and indirectly. A good learning environment is a place that looks and feels exciting, a place that puts youth in touch with the session visually and emotionally as soon as they arrive. Following are some guidelines to follow to have a Bible study space where youth are comfortable.

- A separate classroom is needed for each youth class with an enrollment of 1 to 12 youth. A minimum of 8 to 10 square feet per person in the classroom is needed.

- A separate department room is needed for each youth department with an enrollment of up to 60 youth.

- Youth need chairs with seats 18 inches above the ground. Whenever possible, stacking or folding chairs should be used. Provide only enough chairs for expected attendance.

- Folding tables in six and eight-foot lengths are best for youth Bible studies. Round tables are also good. Tabletops in poor condition should be covered with wood-grain adhesive paper or paper table covers.

- Chalkboards and marker boards are excellent teaching tools, but require care and maintenance. When chalkboards become damaged or scratched, they can be refinished with chalkboard paint available from teacher/school supply stores. Special cleaners are available for marker boards to make them look like new. If a classroom has neither, large pieces of paper and felt-tip markers may be used. (A free-standing, rolling chalkboard is also an option.)

- Cork bulletin boards provide an ideal surfacr for tacking and stapling posters, banners, and other visuals. Masking tape or a plastic putty may be used on walls to make a focal wall in the room.

- Every department needs an area for storing supplies, curriculum, and other reference resources. Store books, extra Bibles, and hymnals on open shelving; include reference books that will help youth discover answers for themselves—Bible dictionary, Bible atlas, concordances, commentaries, and so on. Felt-tip and white board markers, pencils, scissors, and other art supplies may be kept in a storage closet or cabinet. Stack paper neatly so it may be easily accessed from the shelves. A roll of butcher comes in handy, if there is room to store it or mount it on a wall.

- Today's youth live in a visual world. Youth Sunday School can make good use of a television set and VCR on a rolling cart for viewing segments of movies or Christian music videos. A C/cassette tape boombox can provide Christian music as youth arrive on Sunday mornings.

YOUTH SUNDAY SCHOOL JOB DESCRIPTIONS

Student Leader

Youth who serve as student leaders should:

- be disciples and conduct themselves in a way that honors God.
- witness to peers, lead them to faith in Jesus Christ, and church membership.
- help plan, promote, and participate in fellowship opportunities; encourage group members to participate in building fellowship.
- assist the teacher in reaching youth through personal and group visitation and encourage the involvement of class members in personal visitation and group outreach events.
- be personally involved in the Bible studies, encourage peers to be personally involved, and enlist class members to accept assignments in the Bible studies.
- maintain a personal quiet time, participate in corporate worship, and encourage other youth to do the same.
- assist the teacher in leading the class, and serve as a link between the teacher and class members. (Occasionally, the class leader should participate in weekly leadership meetings.)
- be a member of a Student FAITH team, if in a FAITH church.

Teacher

A teacher's responsibility is:

- to live by the principle that the leader is the lesson and Sunday School is a seven-day-a-week strategy.
- to administer the growth of a Youth Sunday School class by planning weekly for effective Bible study, and to participate in training opportunities.
- to evangelize youth and the adults who influence them through regular contacts, participation in personal visitation, and class outreach events.
- to disciple teenagers in their relationship with God and to enlist and train youth to serve as class leaders.
- to guide youth to fellowship with each other as well as with the entire church.
- to minister to teens and their families and to lead youth to care for one another.
- to lead youth to worship by helping them develop a lifestyle that includes personal quiet times and participation in corporate worship.
- to teach youth the Bible using a variety of teaching-learning approaches and prayerfully guiding youth toward spiritual transformation.

Department Director

In addition to the teacher's responsibilities, a department director:

- participates in the growth of Youth Sunday School in the church through annual planning, communication, organization, and evaluation of the work of the department; leads weekly leadership meetings.
- works with the department outreach-evangelism director and/or division director to plan department outreach events for youth and leaders.
- guides the department (large group) time during Sunday School. The department director also relates the department's training needs to the Youth Division Director.
- plans evangelism training opportunities for department members.and leads all members of the department to become involved in witnessing to the unsaved.
- promotes fellowship among youth class members and others on the leadership team by planning quarterly fellowship opportunities.
- encourages youth and leaders to develop personal quiet times and participate in corporate worship, including leading department worship experiences.

[FLIP]

Department Outreach-Evangelism Leader

The department outreach-evangelism leader's job responsibilities include:

- administering the planning and conducting of department outreach and evangelism activities through annual planning events, communication, and weekly leadership meetings.
- evangelizing youth through participation in personal visitation and group outreach events and equipping all other Youth Sunday School members and leaders in developing their evangelism skills.
- functioning as a leader in Student FAITH, if the church is a FAITH church;
- ministering to leaders, members, and nonmembers, and leading youth and leaders to care for members and nonmembers and their families.

Department Secretary

The responsibilities of this job include:

- to process and maintain department records and to compile reports for department leaders.
- to reach and witness to youth and their families through participation in personal visitation and group outreach events, to process and maintain visitation records, to maintain an up-to-date prospect file.
- to participate in weekly leadership meetings by providing record information.
- to maintain all department supplies, including ordering and distributing periodicals.

Division Director

(The youth minister may, in some cases, serve as division director.) The responsibilities include:

- to coordinate the work of multiple departments, guiding them to set goals, and evaluate progress.
- to coordinate annual planning, communication, training opportunities, and generally coordinate the work of youth department directors and any youth division-level leaders.
- to lead the youth division to develop and maintain an effective evangelism strategy.
- to promote fellowship among youth and the leadership team, and among the adult members of the leadership team.
- to plan and participate in ministry to youth leaders, youth, and the families of youth.
- to lead all or part of the weekly leadership meetings.
- to teach as a substitute when needed, to stay in touch with the needs of youth, and to serve as a model for other Youth Sunday School leaders; to plan special youth Bible study groups and projects (Youth Vacation Bible School, Youth January Bible Study, and so forth).
- to communicate regularly with the minister of youth to plan, organize, evaluate, and conduct the work of Youth Sunday School.
- to lead youth to worship by coordinating the planning, training, and implementation of emphases that encourage personal quiet times and participation in corporate worship.

Youth Minister

Sunday School responsibilities of the minister of youth include:

- providing administrative support and resources, including budget, for Youth Sunday School leaders.
- participating in personal visitation and group outreach events; equipping youth and leaders to become involved in evangelizing the unsaved.
- modeling sound Youth Sunday School methods and principles in all training opportunities for members of the Youth Sunday School leadership team.
- promoting fellowship among the youth and the youth leadership team.
- ministering to leaders, members, nonmembers, and their families, and leading youth and leaders to minister to members, nonmembers, and their families.
- discipling youth by helping them develop personal quiet times and participation in corporate worship; involving youth and Youth Sunday School leaders in planning and conducting special youth worship opportunities.

THREE ESSENTIALS OF BIBLE TEACHING FOR SPIRITUAL TRANSFORMATION

PREPARE
the ministry environment

Sunday School Leadership Meeting
- Focus on the Mission
- Focus on Relationships
- Focus on Bible Study

Personal Bible Study

ENCOUNTER
God's Word in a Bible Study group

CONTINUE
Teaching-learning in daily living and family relationships

Motivate youth to study the Bible

Acknowledge Authority
(control)

Examine the Bible Passage

Search the Truth
(content)

Discover the Truth
(concept)

Apply the Bible to Life

Personalize the Truth
(context)

Struggle with the Truth
(conflict)

Believe the Truth
(conviction)

Obey the Truth
(conduct)

Spiritual transformation is God's work of changing a believer into the likeness of Jesus by creating a new identity in Christ and by empowering a lifelong relationship of love, trust, and obedience to glorify God.

SEVEN YOUTH BIBLE TEACHING ELEMENTS

The following chart is representative, not exhaustive, of possible approaches to teaching and learning for youth. For a description of these terms, see chapter 6, "Teaching for Spiritual Transformation."

Seven Bible Teaching Elements	Approaches to Teaching-Learning and Possible Methods Teachers Can Use
Acknowledge Authority	**Relational:** Do impromptu skit on parent-teen issue. **Musical:** Identify key words from a contemporary song or traditional hymn that relates to the session. **Logical:** Youth respond to a series of if/then statements.
Search the Truth	**Natural:** Youth can hold in their hands a stone as they read passage about what Jesus said about casting the first stone (John 8) **Physical:** Perform a skit to portray the parable of the Good Samaritan.
Discover the Truth	**Reflective:** Record in a personal journal the abiding truth from the Scripture passage. **Visual:** Illustrate the abiding truth they found in the Scripture passage.
Personalize the Truth	**Verbal:** Share a personal story of how you personalized the biblical truth. **Relational:** Discuss personal consequences of disobedience and benefits of obedience to the biblical truth.
Struggle with the Truth	**Musical:** Analyze the lyrics of a song to identify the extent to which they identify with a songwriter's struggle with a biblical truth. **Logical:** Rank in order of importance best responses to putting into practice a biblical truth.
Believe the Truth	**Natural:** Observe the night sky or a video of nature to identify which parts of creation reveal a characteristic of God. **Physical:** Move to a continuum line to position yourself on what you believe is the best way to obey a truth.
Obey the Truth	**Reflective:** Set aside a certain time each day for quiet time. **Visual:** Create a visual tract to communicate the biblical truth. **Verbal:** Report to a family member what God has taught you.

CHOOSING CURRICULUM

Curriculum refers to the course, track, or path on which a person runs. Curriculum is similar to running a race toward a finish line, much as the author of Hebrews encouraged his readers to "run with perseverance the race marked out for us" (Heb. 12:1). Note that Hebrews 12:1 calls for the race to be run "with perseverance" and that the race is on a track that is "marked out for us." Choosing Bible study curriculum means pursuing the course that the Bible sets for life—Christlikeness, transformation into the image of Christ (2 Cor. 3:18; Rom. 8:28-29).

Sunday School curriculum is the continuous course, process, or system for Bible study groups to use in order to guide unbelievers toward faith in Christ and believers toward Christlikeness through the transformational power of the Holy Spirit. Sometimes curriculum can be a sprint, like a 100-meter dash—a short course. Ultimately, however, curriculum should be viewed as a marathon, for in the final analysis the track of study the leader and learners choose shapes people's worldview.

Get on the Right Curriculum Track

What principles should you use to select or develop an ongoing curriculum plan, and why will such a plan keep you on an exciting and fruitful curriculum track?

1. When choosing a curriculum plan, choose one that covers all of the Bible's content, not just selected or "favorite" parts. "All Scripture," Paul wrote, "is . . . profitable for teaching, for reproof, for correction, and for training in righteousness" (2 Tim. 3:16). That is, make sure the curriculum plan is comprehensive of all of the Bible and all of life concerns that people face over a specified length of time.

2. Then choose a plan that has a balance of biblical content, Bible study approaches, and life issues. Why not just choose whatever youth want to study, or whatever the "hot topic" or "felt need" is? By following a systematic, comprehensive plan, ongoing Bible study points repeatedly to the fact that the Bible, not developmental life needs and human issues, must guide and shape believers' lives. If a Sunday School leader selects studies that only address youth needs and issues, then the leader risks supplanting the Bible's goal for believers with contemporary perceptions of age-group needs and issues. Occasional topical, issue-oriented studies are necessary and included in ongoing curriculum plans, but the ultimate goal of the Bible and Sunday School curriculum is to lead people toward faith in Christ and transformation toward Christlikeness.

While He was responsive to immediate physical, emotional, and spiritual needs, Jesus didn't always teach on subjects the people wanted—their "felt needs." Jesus was aware there were deeper issues of the human heart that went beyond the current issues of the day—ceremonial washing of hands, Sabbath laws, and getting caught in adultery. Jesus' curriculum plan focused on redemption, the cross, and transformation of human lives beginning with the human heart.

3. Check to see if the curriculum plan is properly sequenced so that learners can build on what they already know. A systematic approach to Bible study facilitates the integration of biblical truth into the learner's life as a life-long ongoing process. Jesus built on what His hearers already knew and took them to a new level when He said, "You have heard that it was said . . . But I tell you . . ." (Matt. 5:43-44).

Remember that spiritual transformation into Christlikeness is a life-long process. Because curriculum is best viewed from the perspective of a marathon, appropriate repetition of biblical content and life concerns in different ways and at different times strengthens learners, much as a fresh cup of water reinvigorates a marathon runner. The Hebrews 12:1 principle of perseverance for believers applies here. At the same time, "open" Bible study groups will always have new people joining the curriculum race—new learners who'll need the basics the veteran learners could help teach. Do a quick survey of Jesus' teaching in the Gospels, and you'll discover how frequently He repeated themes—and how slowly His disciples caught on.

A properly sequenced Bible study plan is one expression of the principle of "renewing the mind" found in Romans 12:2. Isn't the ministry of the Holy Spirit to help believers recall what Jesus taught and to help believers become "experts" in living and bearing witness for Christ?

4. A planned, ongoing Bible study strategy is most conducive to creating a ministry environment that fosters strong relationships and regularly invites the lost to believe in Christ. Ongoing groups have a more fixed organizational structure that provide more stable leadership over a longer period of time. A ministry environment of grace and acceptance takes time for God to create.

[FLIP]

In addition, one important aspect of creating a ministry environment is helping prepare the participants to hear God's message for a particular time. A planned, ongoing Bible study strategy is a wise discipline for the person who wants to hear God speak and is seeking to obey God's direction. By submitting to a disciplined, lifelong approach to listening to God through His written Word, we do not presume to know exactly what God would speak to us. Instead we demonstrate a commitment to love God and His Word—all of it; to trust God and His Word—all of it; and to obey God and His Word—all of it. Teaching and studying an ongoing, well-designed curriculum plan demonstrates a heart that is ready to be transformed.

With regard to curriculum planning or "curriculum mapping," God knows the timeliness of any study for any individual's life as well as for a people's time and circumstances. Through the leadership of the Holy Spirit, He will guide those He has placed in strategic places of leadership in discerning the lessons and messages He has for those who will receive them. Curriculum planners carry a tremendous accountability to actively seek God's direction; and then to receive, and faithfully obey His direction.

The Holy Spirit can work in the hearts of curriculum planners months and years in advance to design studies that are truly God's message for a particular time. Those who design comprehensive, balanced, and properly sequenced Bible study plans will always seek to hear God's voice to choose Bible studies that help believers come face-to-face with God's message in order for them to take it to their communities, culture, and world.

Choose the Best Curriculum Resources

With regard to the curriculum resources, make sure the resources you choose express the curriculum plan that meets these four principles and accomplishes the ministry goals you and your church believe God wants you to fulfill. Materials produced by LifeWay Christian Resources contain Bible study curriculum plans that are comprehensive, balanced, properly sequenced, and conducive to ongoing ministry and address the 1-5-4 principle of Kingdom Growth to build Great Commission Christians. In addition, LifeWay curriculum resources, whether print, video, audio, electronic, or multimedia:

- guide churches to fulfill the Great Commission through the five essential functions for church growth—evangelism, discipleship, ministry, fellowship, and worship.
- provide sound, reliable interpretation of the Bible from a conservative point of view.
- offer clear support for evangelism, including the FAITH Sunday School Evangelism Strategy.
- provide a variety of age-appropriate, timely, and relevant teaching-learning approaches, all of which lead learners toward faith in Christ and spiritual transformation into Christlikeness.
- supplement teaching-learning plans with resource kits and leader packs containing creative posters and teaching aids and free on-line "EXTRA! Teaching Helps" containing the latest news, research, and other ideas on the Internet web site, www.lifeway.com.
- provide choices of Bible study options that feature comprehensive, balanced, sequenced, and ministry-conducive curriculum.
- offer a variety of reasonably priced, easy-to-use, and attractive learner and leader resources in print, audio, electronic, and/or multimedia formats
- feature biblical insights and teaching approaches written by Southern Baptists experienced in Sunday School work in the churches.
- provide financial assistance to the Cooperative Program for various Southern Baptist ministries through the sale of Bible study resources.
- offer an optional devotional and reading guide to deepen their daily commitment to love, trust, and obey God based on the Bible study participants study on Sunday.
- contain leader, teacher, and learner development features to engage and equip every one in the full ministry of evangelism, discipleship, ministry, fellowship, and worship through Sunday School.

Think carefully about which track you want to run on . . . and then *run with perseverance the race marked out for us* (Heb. 12:1).

APPROACHES TO LEARNING & TEACHING FOR YOUTH*

*This chart is representative, not exhaustive, of possible approaches to learning and teaching for youth.

RELATIONAL Barnabas	MUSICAL David	LOGICAL Paul	NATURAL David	PHYSICAL Ezekiel	REFLECTIVE Mary	VISUAL John	VERBAL Solomon
Learners Clarify -Leaders can ask youth, "What does this mean to you?"	Learners Listen - Leaders can play a contemporary Christian song and ask youth to listen to what the song says.	Learners Organize - Leaders can ask youth, "How can we address this problem? What can we do, who can do it, and when?"	Learners Dig/Touch - Leaders can introduce youth to the role of the sacrificial lamb by letting them observe a live lamb.	Learners Touch - Leaders can ask youth to join hands to form a circle to symbolize unity.	Learners Meditate - Leaders can encourage youth to think about things for which they are thankful.	Learners Create a Montage Leaders can ask youth to create a montage from magazine photographs of people with great needs.	Learners Listen - Leaders can tell youth the story of Mary and Martha.
Learners Affirm - Leaders can encourage youth to write a note to an adult who has been a help and support to them.	Learners Record - Leaders can provide a cassette recorder for youth to record songs, choral readings, and so forth.	Learners Compare/Contrast - Leaders can guide youth to contrast the fruit of the Spirit with the acts of the sinful nature.	Learners Sort/Classify - Leaders can ask youth to separate items into what God made and what people have made.	Learners Recreate - Leaders can guide youth to build a rock alter (like Jacob did) to mark a commitment they made to follow God.	Learners Evaluate Themselves Leaders can ask youth to identify one weakness in their prayer lives.	Learners Observe - Leaders can direct youth to watch a videotaped case study, following this with a discussion or written response.	Learners Paraphrase - Leaders can ask youth to rewrite and tell the parable of the lost coins in a modern-day version.
Learners Empathize - Leaders can ask youth: "How do you think Jonathan felt knowing David would be king and not him?"	Learners Sing - Leaders can lead youth in singing "Awesome God" as a response to Psalm 8.	Learners Reason - Leaders can ask youth to respond to a series of *if/then* statements.	Learners Observe - Leaders can ask youth to observe a scientific demonstration and explain how it shows order in the universe.	Learners Act/Dramatize - Leaders can ask youth to act out a role play that demonstrates the principle of forgiveness.	Learners Contemplate - Leaders can ask youth to consider possible results of a particular mistake in their lives.	Learners Diagram – Leaders can ask youth to sketch what they think the temple might have looked like based on the Bible's descriptions of the temple.	Learners List - Leaders can ask youth to make a list of the Ten Commandments.
Learners Mediate - Leaders can ask youth to role play a conflict and discuss how to resolve the conflict.	Learners Compose - Leaders can ask youth to compose a song or rap that expresses the truth of the focal passage.	Learners Analyze - Leaders can ask youth, "Why do people act that way? What happens to a Christian who continues to act that way?"	Learners Protect - Leaders can guide youth to create and implement a project that reflects Christian stewardship of creation.	Learners Move - Leaders can ask youth to move to the appropriate agree/disagree poster, based on their opinions of certain statements.	Learners Log - Leaders can have youth track the amount of time they spend this week watching television and in prayer.	Learners Draw/Illustrate - Leaders can instruct youth to illustrate on a large sheet of paper areas where youth often feel tempted.	Learners Write Ideas - Leaders can ask youth to write a note to a senior adult member of the church.
Learners Question - Leaders can encourage youth to ask one another how they would respond to the case study.	Learners Evaluate Music - Leaders can ask youth to describe how the music made them feel.	Learners Evaluate - Leaders can show a video and ask youth to identify appropriate and inappropriate responses of characters to various situations.	Learners Reflect - Leaders can help youth identify principles of science that point to an orderly Creator.	Learners Create - Leaders can instruct youth to use chenille strips and create something that symbolizes something they can do for God.	Learners Write in Journals - Leaders can guide youth to keep a journal on ways they have experienced God's presence during the week.	Learners Demonstrate - Leaders can ask youth to show the results of their work during the class time.	Learners Use Humor/Stories - Leaders can ask youth to give humorous examples similar to Jesus' example of the plank and speck of dust.
Learners Respond - Leaders can instruct youth to list ways they could help a local ministry or mission project.	Learners Respond to Music - Leaders can ask youth to decide how music influences them.	Learners Rank - Leaders can ask youth to compare items and list them in order of their importance.	Learners Collect/Display - Leaders can ask youth to bring examples of environmental pollution.	Learners Manipulate - Leaders can guide youth to rearrange the letters each of them is holding to create the Key Verse.	Learners Study - Leaders can ask youth to read the Focal Passage and answer questions about it.	Learners Propose - Leaders can ask youth to describe what they think Jesus might have seen when He looked out over the crowds while He hung on the cross.	Learners Report - Leaders can instruct youth to research the meaning of key words used in a passage and report findings to the class.
Learners Discuss - Leaders can guide youth to discuss possible consequences of disobeying those in authority.	Learners Play Instruments - Leaders can encourage youth to play instruments and lead the group in singing choruses.	Learners Classify - Leaders can display pictures of youth in different situations and direct youth to tell which pictures show ministry in action.	Learners Identify - Leaders can ask youth to clip photos or illustrations of items discovered in Holy Land excavations.	Learners Play in Sports - Leaders can encourage youth to use a basketball game to exhibit Christlikeness and open the door to witnessing.	Learners Personalize - Leaders can ask youth to assume the role of a biblical character in a given situation and identify how the person might have responded.	Learners Paint – Leaders can guide youth to design and paint a "billboard" that presents the gospel.	Learners Label - Leaders can call out various things and direct youth to say if they are wants or needs.
Learners Dialogue - Leaders can ask youth open-ended questions like, "How would you complete this sentence?"	Learners Adapt/Create - Leaders can direct youth to create new verses to a chorus that expresses things for which they are thankful.	Learners Graph - Leaders can guide youth to make a graph of their lives, showing high and low points in their walk with Christ.	Learners Plant/Cultivate - Leaders can lead youth to discuss the nature of faith by planting seeds and watching their growth over the months.	Learners Display - Leaders can ask youth to bring seemingly unrelated items to assemble in class to show how parts become the whole.	Learners Intuit - Leaders can ask youth to consider what God is directing them to do as a result of this study.	Learners Storyboard - Leaders can guide youth to create a six-panel cartoon that gives the main action of the story.	Learners Recite - Leaders can assign a psalm for youth to use in developing a dramatic monologue or responsive reading.

Teaching Plan for *Youth Sunday School for a New Century*

By Ann Cannon

Use this two and one-half-hour plan as a guide for planning a group study of *Youth Sunday School for A New Century.* You may conduct an all-day study or several shorter training sessions. However you choose to study this book, read the contents with a commitment to make 21st century Youth Sunday School work the best ever.

Before the Session

- Gather name tags, large sheets of paper or poster board, felt-tip markers, pencils, masking tape, and Bibles.
- Provide copies of *Youth Sunday School for a New Century* to be used during the session.
- Gather items for Step 1. Duplicate "Get in Touch With Today's Youth," page 16.
- For step 2, post a large sheet of paper labeled "New Century Teenagers" on a focal wall.
- For step 3, make an overhead cel of the new Sunday School definition from the appendix. If you don't have an overhead projector, make copies for distribution.
- For step 3, write the five functions of Evangelism, Discipleship, Fellowship, Ministry, Worship on separate large strips of paper. List the "Ten Best Practices" (pages 8-9) on another sheet of paper.

During the Session

- **Step 1** (10 min.)–As youth leaders arrive, ask each to make a name tag. Hand each leader a copy of the "Get in Touch With Today's Youth" handout and a pencil. Direct them to walk around, introduce themselves, and discuss with other leaders possible answers to the questions. If possible, provide several magazines youth read, listings of top ten songs youth listen to (get these lists from a local music store), movie pages from newspapers, television guides, and pictures of youth wearing current fashion fads (advertisements are helpful) . As you begin, direct leaders to keep these response sheets until later in the session.

- **Step 2** (15 min.)–Say: Going into a new century everyone has great hope for something fresh and positive. As you think about the new century, what is your heart's desire–your passion–for new century teenagers? Write responses on the large sheet of paper. Say: Now, think about Youth Sunday School for the new century. What is your heart's desire–your passion–for your new century Youth Sunday School? List responses as a second column headed "New Century Youth Sunday School." Read Psalm 37:4 aloud. Lead in prayer asking God for wisdom and guidance in finding ways to gain our heart's desires.

- **Step 3** (15 min.)–Say: Everyone's curious about what the 21st century will bring. *What will happen to Youth Sunday School?* Will it self-destruct like a Y2K problem because leaders aren't adjusting to the new generation of teenagers? Will it continue with the same old things? Or, will it look different, feel different, and be more effective? One thing won't change–the driving impetus for Youth Sunday School is still Matthew 28:18-20. Read these verses aloud. or call on a conferee to read. Display the new definition of Sunday School as an overhead cel or hand out copies to conferees. Emphasize these points:

1. Sunday School is a strategy, not an organization. This broadens the opportunities for Bible study beyond one hour on Sunday morning. Youth Sunday School is a 24/7 (24-hours-a-day, seven-day-a-week) strategy for reaching new teenagers for Jesus Christ and discipling those who have already made a commitment.
2. The five functions (or purposes) of Sunday School are identified in the definition–evangelism, discipleship, fellowship, ministry, and worship. Using Chapter 1 of *Youth Sunday School for A New Century,* explain each function as you reveal the paper with that function written on it. State that during this session leaders will determine how these functions can happen in Youth Sunday School.
3. Point out that strategies and functions must go beyond the theoretical to the practical. State that *Youth Sunday School for A New Century* presents the ten best practices for making Youth Sunday School happen. Post the "Ten Best Practices" list next to the lists of "New Century Teenagers" and "New Century Youth Sunday School." Point out similarities.

- **Step 4** (50 min.)–Say: Let's look at specifics from this "Ten Best Practices" list. Divide leaders into five teams. Give each team paper, markers, and copies of *Youth Sunday School for A New Century.* Assign each team one chapter, Chapters 2 through 6. Direct teams to prepare a poster that expresses the major content of their assigned chapter. Offer these suggestions for their posters. Leaders could:

*design a poster with a center theme and FAQs (Frequently Asked Questions) around it like spokes of a wheel.

*draw stick figures in several scenes that review the contents and could be used as a storyboard for a video.

*select a key word or phrase and build an acrostic off of it.

*cut the poster apart and prepare several banners, each highlighting a major point in the assigned chapter.

*design a website based on the chapter information.

Allow 20 minutes to work and 5 minutes to report. Suggest that different people on each team read a segment of the team's assigned chapter, then combine their information in creating the poster.

After a 10-minute break, call for team reports. As each team reports, point out related pages from the appendix in the back of the book. If FAQs are asked on a poster, be sure they are also answered. After all teams have reported, ask each team to share the implications of how the information in their assigned chapter impacts their heart's desire lists from step 2.

• **Step 5** (30 min.)—Continue in the five teams formed in Step 4. Display the overhead cel used in step 3 or refer to the handouts with the definition. Stress that Sunday School is a strategy. Say: If Sunday School is a strategy, not an organization, the principles that form this strategy are important. Direct leaders to "Five Strategic Principles" on pages 7-8. Assign each team one principle. Point out the icon related to each principle. Say: Let's look at how these principles are foundational to Youth Sunday School. In each chapter look for the icon related to your assigned principle. This indicates that your assigned principle supports the information in that part of the chapter. Point out that there are many other places throughout the book where these principles are evident. The icons highlight *some* of these places. Using the explanations under each principle, decide which of the four points is supported.

* Instruct each team to look through the book and find examples of at least two of the four points under their assigned strategic principle, reminding them that they may find examples other places than those designated by the icons. Call for reports.

Say: These principles support all you do in Youth Sunday School. They are the backbone, the foundation. Our tendency is to think that Youth Sunday School is only about teaching. You've seen that there are many other areas. Teaching is a part of the process, but not the whole process. (At this point you may want to offer a stand-up break.)

Step 6 (25 min.)—As leaders return to their seats, direct them to Chapter 6 (p. 55) in *Youth Sunday School for A New Century.* Say: Some things won't change in new century Youth Sunday School. (*The Bible as the textbook; a sense of calling to lead youth; the charge to make disciples in Matthew 28:19-20; the desire to work with God to transform a teenager's life.*) Ask: What does change in new century Youth Sunday School? After several answers, share these ideas from Chapter 6.

• Explain that starting with curriculum developed after the year 2000, terminology will be different. "Prepare" will be the opening information, similar to a motivational step; "Encounter" will be the opportunity for Bible study and its application to life; "Continue" will carry that application into life beyond the Bible study period.

• Point out the new meanings to familiar terms as expressed in "Second, Encounter!" on pages 59-60. Emphasize that strong application reaches this generation of teenagers.

• If leaders have Bibles, direct them to look up either Luke 22:1-38, Luke 9:57-59, or Matthew 26:30. Point out the teaching-learning approaches on pages 60-61. Ask leaders to quickly find the different teaching-learning approaches Jesus used. Say: Teenagers today are bombarded with many images at once, and they have extensive technology available to them. Written words on a page can't compete unless we use variety and inventive ways of expressing those words. Point out how "Extra!" as explained on page 64 is another way of updating curriculum. Offer to talk after the session with anyone who has questions about which curriculum to use.

Step 7 (5 min.)—Hand out sheets of paper. Direct attention to the "Ten Best Practices" list displayed in step 3. Ask leaders to number their papers from one to ten . Tell them to give themselves a grade beside each of the best practices. Challenge leaders to write down one statement from the heart's desire lists ("New Century Teenagers" or "New Century Youth Sunday School") as a goal or prayer they have for their situation. Encourage leaders to use what they've learned today in making their Youth Sunday School capable of spiritually transforming teenagers in the new century.

Read 1 Corinthians 15:58 as a closing challenge and prayer.

CHRISTIAN GROWTH STUDY PLAN

Preparing Christians to Serve

In the **Christian Growth Study Plan (formerly Church Study Course),** this book **Youth Sunday School for a New Century** is a resource for course credit in **two** Leadership and Skill Development diploma plans. To receive credit, read the book, complete the learning activities, show your work to your pastor, a staff member or church leader, then complete the following information. This page may be duplicated. Send the completed page to:

Christian Growth Study Plan
127 Ninth Avenue, North, MSN 117
Nashville, TN 37234-0117
FAX: (615)251-5067

For information about the Christian Growth Study Plan, refer to the current Christian Growth Study Plan Catalog. Your church office may have a copy. If not, request a free copy from the Christian Growth Study Plan office (615/251-2525).

COURSE CREDIT INFORMATION

Please check the appropriate box indicating the diploma you want to apply this credit. You may check more than one.

- ❑ **The Administration of Youth Ministries (LS-0025)**
- ❑ **Leadership Development of the Associational Leader (LS-0068)**

PARTICIPANT INFORMATION

Social Security Number (USA Only)	Personal CGSP Number*	Date of Birth (Mo., Day, Yr.)
___-__-____	____-___-___	__-__-__

Name (First, MI, Last) ❑Mr. ❑Miss ❑Mrs. ❑	Home Phone
	___-___-____

Address (Street, Route, or P.O. Box)	City, State, or Province	Zip/Postal Code

CHURCH INFORMATION

Church Name		
Address (Street, Route, or P.O. Box)	City, State, or Province	Zip/Postal Code

CHANGE REQUEST ONLY

❑Former Name		
❑Former Address	City, State, or Province	Zip/Postal Code
❑Former Church	City, State, or Province	Zip/Postal Code

Signature of Pastor, Conference Leader, or Other Church Leader	Date

***New participants are requested but not required to give SS# and date of birth. Existing participants, please give CGSP# when using SS# for the first time. Thereafter, only one ID# is required. *Mail To:* Christian Growth Study Plan, 127 Ninth Ave., North, MSN 117, Nashville, TN 37234-0117. Fax: (615)251-5067**